INCLUSIVE, BALANCED, SUSTAINED GROWTH IN THE ASIA PACIFIC

The **Pacific Economic Cooperation Council (PECC)** is one of the Asia-Pacific's most influential organizations. Since its foundation in 1980 it has been a policy innovator in trade, finance, information technology and capacity-building, among others. PECC brings together leading thinkers and decision-makers from government and business in an informal setting to discuss and formulate ideas on the most significant issues facing the Asia-Pacific. PECC is the only non-government official observer in APEC. For more details visit http://www.pecc.org.

The **Institute of Southeast Asian Studies (ISEAS)** was established as an autonomous organization in 1968. It is a regional centre dedicated to the study of socio-political, security and economic trends and developments in Southeast Asia and its wider geostrategic and economic environment. The Institute's research programmes are the Regional Economic Studies (RES, including ASEAN and APEC), Regional Strategic and Political Studies (RSPS), and Regional Social and Cultural Studies (RSCS).

ISEAS Publishing, an established academic press, has issued more than 2,000 books and journals. It is the largest scholarly publisher of research about Southeast Asia from within the region. ISEAS Publishing works with many other academic and trade publishers and distributors to disseminate important research and analyses from and about Southeast Asia to the rest of the world.

INCLUSIVE, BALANCED, SUSTAINED GROWTH IN THE ASIA PACIFIC

EDITED BY
PETER A. PETRI

PACIFIC ECONOMIC COOPERATION COUNCIL
TASKFORCE ON THE GLOBAL ECONOMIC CRISIS

INSTITUTE OF SOUTHEAST ASIAN STUDIES
SINGAPORE

First published in Singapore in 2010 by
ISEAS Publishing
Institute of Southeast Asian Studies
30 Heng Mui Keng Terrace
Pasir Panjang
Singapore 119614

E-mail: publish@iseas.edu.sg
Website: http://bookshop.iseas.edu.sg

ISEAS Library Cataloguing-in-Publication Data

Inclusive, balanced, sustained growth in the Asia-Pacific / edited by Peter A. Petri.
1. Asia—Economic conditions.
2. Asia—Economic policy.
3. Pacific Area—Economic conditions.
4. Pacific Area—Economic policy.
I. Petri, Peter A., 1946–
II. Pacific Economic Cooperation Council. Task Force on the Global Economic Crisis.

HC412 I36   2010

ISBN 978-981-230-966-2 (soft cover)
ISBN 978-981-4279-77-2 (E-Book PDF)

Typeset by Superskill Graphics Pte Ltd
Printed in Singapore by Photoplates Pte Ltd

Contents

Preface

As the global economic crisis intensified in March 2009, the Pacific Economic Cooperation Council (PECC) organized a workshop on "Regional Responses to the Economic Crisis" hosted by the Japan Committee for Pacific Economic Cooperation in Osaka, Japan. The meeting concluded that the Asia-Pacific faced historic challenges that call for unprecedented policy responses, cooperation and analysis.

To address these challenges, the PECC created a Taskforce on the Global Economic Crisis to "assess the region's progress in fighting recession, rebalancing economic structures, and managing sustained recoveries ... [and to] anticipate the critical policy changes that will be required in the Asia Pacific to move from crisis management to stable growth." Recognizing that the International Monetary Fund and the World Bank and other institutions were already contributing timely information on global developments, the PECC Standing Committee concluded that value could be added by providing independent analysis of policy options with particular emphasis on regional responses in the Asia-Pacific, where several key economies involved in the crisis are located. I was asked to chair the Taskforce.

Over the next few weeks we assembled a team of seven experts — an international group of leading researchers — and developed an ambitious work programme to produce results in less than six months, given the urgency of the crisis. We invited several other distinguished experts to serve as a "Panel of Advisers" (listed below). We discussed preliminary findings at a conference on "The Global Economic Crisis: Macroeconomic Issues", hosted by the Asian Development Bank Institute in Tokyo on 28–29 July 2009 and an advanced draft at a conference on the "Economic Crisis and Recovery: Enhancing Resilience, Structural Reform, and Freer Trade in the Asia-Pacific Region", hosted by the Singapore National Committee for Pacific Economic Cooperation and the Institute of Policy Studies in Singapore on 9–10 October 2009.

Comments at both conferences provided essential guidance for the study and helped to improve this report.

A preliminary summary of the report appeared as Chapter 1 of PECC's *State of the Region Report 2009–2010* and was presented to participants at the APEC Leaders' Meeting in November 2009. We are hopeful that work within APEC will find these recommendations useful and build on them.

The team is grateful to Drs Charles Morrison and Jusuf Wanandi, PECC Co-Chairs, and the PECC Standing Committee for encouragement and support. The Taskforce's Advisers provided highly valuable input on research plans and intermediate drafts. We hesitate to single out individuals, but Jonathan Fried, Ambassador of Canada to Japan, and his colleagues provided especially detailed and insightful comments at several stages. We are grateful to the Asian Development Bank Institute and its Dean Masahiro Kawai, Mario Lamberte, Research Director, and Peter Morgan, for hosting our planning efforts. Eduardo Pedrosa, the Secretary General of PECC and Jessica Yom of the Secretariat provided outstanding support for the project, promoted it actively and successfully, and brought this publication to fruition.

Peter A. Petri
Chair, PECC Taskforce on the Global Economic Crisis

Taskforce on the Global Economic Crisis

Peter A. PETRI (Chair, U.S.)
Professor, Brandeis University and East-West Center

Yongfu CAO (China)
Assistant Research Fellow, Chinese Academy of Social Sciences

Wendy DOBSON (Canada)
Professor, University of Toronto

Yiping HUANG (China)
Professor, Peking University and Australian National University

Michael PLUMMER (U.S.)
Professor, Johns Hopkins University and East-West Center

Raimundo SOTO (Chile)
Associate Professor, Pontificia Universidad Catolica de Chile

Shinji TAKAGI (Japan)
Professor, Osaka University

Panel of Advisers

Dr Siow Yue CHIA (Singapore)
Singapore Institute of International Affairs

Professor Barry EICHENGREEN (U.S.)
University of California, Berkeley

Professor Christopher FINDLAY (Australia)
University of Adelaide

Ambassador Jonathan FRIED (Canada)
Ambassador of Canada to Japan

Dean Masahiro KAWAI (Japan)
Asian Development Bank Institute

Dr Jong-Wha LEE (Korea)
Asian Development Bank

Professor Yung Chul PARK (Korea)
Seoul National University

Professor Hugh PATRICK (U.S.)
Columbia University

Dr Andrew SHENG (Malaysia)
University of Malaya

Professor Robert SCOLLAY (New Zealand)
University of Auckland

Dr Chalongphob SUSSANGKARN (Thailand)
Thailand Development Research Institute

Professor Shujiro URATA (Japan)
Waseda University

Dr Josef T. YAP (Philippines)
Philippine Institute of Development Studies

Professor Yunling ZHANG (China)
Chinese Academy of Social Sciences

Executive Summary

The recovery of the Asia-Pacific from the global economic crisis of 2008–09 is underway but incomplete. Despite encouraging progress, major risks remain, ranging from slow growth and persistent unemployment to reemerging global imbalances and renewed financial volatility.

The policies that stopped the economic freefall — massive stimulus and financial bailout packages — were urgent, relatively easy to sell politically, and to a large extent forced by circumstances (particularly the fall of Lehman Brothers). Sustained recovery now requires tackling different problems, including international imbalances among the United States, China, and other economies. U.S. consumers are not likely to drive world demand in the medium term, and the slack will have to be taken up in part by Asian consumption and investment. The early policy responses, successful as they were in averting a larger calamity, were not designed to address longer-term issues, and some are even counterproductive from that perspective.

INCLUSIVE, BALANCED, SUSTAINED GROWTH

This report argues that given the progress already made, inclusive, balanced, sustained growth in the region — in other words, full recovery — is feasible. But renewed growth is not assured and calls for new, difficult policy choices. These include structural reforms that change economic relationships within economies and among them. International cooperation will be essential for forging and implementing this strategy.

The term "rebalancing" is now widely applied to policies for sustaining the recovery. This report seeks to bring greater precision to the analysis of these issues, and in particular to policies addressing global imbalances. In 2009, the short-term effects of the crisis brought the current account imbalances of the United States, China and Japan to levels that are generally considered sustainable. But as the recovery proceeds, and assuming no major policy changes, imbalances are again likely to grow. Should markets conclude that imbalances are no longer under control, currency and asset prices would become volatile again, perhaps triggering another downturn.

Avoiding market volatility is one important reason for rebalancing. Providing new drivers for demand, given the expected slow recovery of consumption in the United States and Europe, is another. This will also increase expenditures in emerging economies on consumption and social priorities, helping to make growth more inclusive and to spread more widely the benefits of the region's extraordinary economic gains.

The arithmetic of rebalancing appears manageable. In the run-up to the crisis, the "excessive" part of the U.S. current account deficit (the portion above 3 per cent of GDP) amounted to around 1 per cent of the Asia-Pacific region's GDP. These imbalances, which have exerted great stress on global financial relations, are relatively small when compared to domestic expenditures in large economies. But the arithmetic tells only part of the story; imbalances often reflect deeper distortions within national economies and are therefore politically difficult to solve.

STRUCTURAL POLICIES

The transition to sustained growth will require economies to exit their stimulus programmes and to replace them with structural reforms that drive growth through the recovery and beyond. Although the common effect of these policies will be to generate adequate, balanced, sustainable demand, their details depend on the structural weaknesses of different economies. For example:

- U.S. policies could impose new disciplines on consumer and government spending by reining in excessive borrowing and by increasing taxes.
- China's policies could stimulate domestic demand by improving social safety nets, freeing labour markets in order to raise wages, and opening capital markets to smaller firms.
- Japan and other advanced Asian economies could free up service sectors and refocus technological capabilities on growth markets such as aging populations and energy conservation.
- Southeast Asia and South America could accelerate investment through measures that improve productivity and the conditions for doing business.

If these changes in demand are achieved, they will need to be accompanied by parallel changes in supply. Exchange rate flexibility (the appreciation of the currencies of China and other Asian exporters and depreciation of the U.S. dollar) is the least disruptive way to provide incentives for the required resource transfers.

GROWTH ENGINES

Demand and supply shifts could be further accelerated with high profile Asia-Pacific "growth engines" that address key social and environmental priorities. These could provide a focal point for government investments and incentives, and for support from international institutions such as the Asian Development Bank and the World Bank. Four important areas for such projects are:

- Economic integration: investments in connectivity and trade agreements that strengthen Asia-Pacific markets.
- Green economy: investments in energy conservation, research and development, efficient irrigation, and energy-saving vehicles and transport systems.
- Social priorities: investments in education, health care, pensions and social safety nets.
- Knowledge and productivity: investments in research and development and technology, and reforms to drive productivity.

Such regional initiatives could stimulate Asian demand, create markets for Asia's manufactures, engage American resources and technology, and put Asia's savings to productive use.

A ROLE FOR ASIA-PACIFIC INSTITUTIONS

International cooperation will be essential for inclusive, balanced, sustained growth. The G-20 now provides a "board of directors" for the global system, with substantial Asia-Pacific membership. But the plans of the G-20 will need to be translated into pragmatic initiatives. Asia-Pacific institutions could play a central role in implementing these, for example by orchestrating the realignment of Asian exchange rates (ASEAN+3), by encouraging economic integration and stimulating productivity growth, and by launching engines of growth focused on social and environmental priorities (APEC, ASEAN+6 and others).

Interdependence in the Asia-Pacific is now often viewed as a source of risk, but it connects the most powerful technological, financial, and productive resources ever assembled. The region's institutions should not miss the opportunity to exploit these connections to address the crisis. By working together, Asia-Pacific governments can signal to markets that they are committed to cooperation and will keep growth on track.

1

A Regional Framework for Inclusive, Balanced, Sustained Growth

Yongfu Cao, Wendy Dobson, Yiping Huang, Peter A. Petri, Michael Plummer, Raimundo Soto and Shinji Takagi

I. INTRODUCTION

The Asia-Pacific region is at the forefront of the recovery from the global economic crisis of 2008–09. But despite the region's strong economic fundamentals, major challenges lie ahead in exiting interventions adopted in the crisis and building solid foundations for future growth. There is still ample risk of slow growth and persistent unemployment, reemerging global imbalances, and financial volatility.

The policies that stopped the economic freefall — huge stimulus packages in China, Japan, the United States and even small economies like Singapore, and massive financial bailouts in the West — were urgent, relatively easy to sell politically, and to a large extent forced by circumstances (particularly the fall of Lehman Brothers). They were deployed under extraordinary time pressures and have proved remarkably successful.

But sustained recovery will require tackling different problems, including but not limited to current account imbalances among the United States, China, Japan and other economies. U.S. consumers are not likely to drive world demand in the near future and Asian consumption and investment will have to emerge as new engines of growth. The policies used to fight the crisis, successful as they were in averting a larger calamity, did not directly address this transition and some have been counterproductive from a long-term perspective.

The best outcomes — inclusive, balanced, sustained (IBS) growth — will require shifting the policy mix from crisis intervention to structural reforms. These will need to change economic relationships within economies and among them. The mix will be varied and complex, addressing household and government finances, investment incentives, risk management, infrastructure, productivity, and other fundamental determinants of growth.

The policy mix should also foster new engines of growth in the Asia-Pacific by focusing the region's entrepreneurship, innovation and resources on common priorities. Concerted regional initiatives could, for example, target cleaner and more reliable energy; energy-saving transport and new vehicles; more efficient irrigation; critical public services and social safety nets; and products and services to meet the needs of ageing populations.

This study argues that IBS growth is feasible in the Asia-Pacific. The region's dynamic, emerging economies have led the global recovery and the United States, despite its ailing financial sector, has also turned the corner. Global imbalances are, for now, at acceptable levels and can be kept so with forceful policies. Addressing the key threats to global recovery — weaknesses in financial oversight and limits to growth based on massive international capital flows — are widely considered essential. If actions are now taken to address these threats, the crisis will have ultimately made the world economy stronger and more resilient.

International cooperation has been, and remains, central to the recovery. By articulating a shared strategy for growth, governments can enhance the consistency of policies and the stability of the business environment. They can signal common purpose and commit to holding each other accountable for keeping growth on track. Markets and investors critically depend on such signals in the uncertain aftermath of the crisis.

The G-20, now the premier global consultative mechanism, is a promising platform for cooperation and it gives the Asia-Pacific a voice commensurate with its economic importance. This global process needs to be complemented with regional cooperation. Asia-Pacific institutions — including ASEAN, ASEAN+3, the East Asian Summit, APEC and smaller groups — can add value by translating global goals into executable initiatives. This report, itself the product of region-wide collaboration, explores a coherent regional strategy both from the "top down" and from the "bottom up" in the economies that will have to implement it.

A successful post-crisis strategy calls for putting growth on a sustainable footing by changing the behaviour of governments, firms and households. It calls for leadership, discipline and popular support. Not only academic, business and policy experts, but also citizens need to understand the issues and choices. Assisting such analysis and dialogue is the primary goal of this study.

II. A FRAMEWORK FOR POST-CRISIS GROWTH

The crisis required emergency interventions to prevent financial systems from collapsing and to halt the calamitous decline of economic activity that began in 2008. The post-crisis economy will require policies that prevent future financial meltdowns and sustain medium-term growth. Since the onset of the crisis, much progress has been made on containing the decline, but work on the foundations of sustained growth has just begun.

Policy Challenges

The short-term challenge policy-makers faced in 2008 was to *manage the devastating impact of the crisis*. In days, or at most weeks, they had to deploy policies to rebuild confidence in financial markets and stop spiralling output, income, employment and asset price declines. Most economies met these challenges with remarkable success, but the solutions adopted — massive government expenditures, monetary easing, financial intervention, and bailouts of companies — increase risks for the longer term. The time to unwind these policies is at hand or approaching in most economies.

The long-term challenge economies face is to *achieve inclusive, balanced, sustained growth* consistent with economic potential. In many economies incomes are low and rapid growth remains a critical priority. But it is now widely accepted that income growth must be achieved alongside other goals — it must be inclusive and sustainable too, generating wide welfare gains and controlling negative environmental externalities. The drivers of growth — technological change, investment, and market-friendly economic policies — remain strong throughout the Asia-Pacific. Indeed, some economies could achieve higher growth rates than they have seen since 1997–98. But all this will require policy changes that orient growth in new directions.

The term "rebalancing" is widely but imprecisely used to describe this challenge. Before the crisis, unsustainable borrowing supported high U.S. consumption, while unprecedented savings — including more than half of China's national income — went into unsustainable investments in dollar assets and export industries. These *internal* imbalances in expenditures led to large *international* imbalances in capital flows between the United States and China, Japan and other economies.

Imbalances have shrunk considerably during the crisis, and consumption growth in the United States and Europe is likely to be restrained even in the intermediate term. Asia-Pacific growth will need to depend more on demand in Asia than before. We will argue that the arithmetic of this adjustment is manageable — the U.S. expenditures that need to be replaced by Asian expenditures amount to only around 1 per cent of the region's approximately $30 trillion GDP — even though the necessary policy changes will reach deeply into economic structures and are likely to be politically contentious.

This study, including the sub-regional analyses of subsequent chapters, explores several solutions:

- Structural measures in the United States that encourage more prudent financial behaviour throughout the economy — not only in the financial sector, but also in household and government finances.
- Structural measures in Asia that extend the region's highly productive economic environment to more sectors (such as services), to factor markets (including capital and labour), and to a wider range of transactions among regional economies.
- New "engines of growth" that address critical social and environmental priories.

Together, these approaches would shift demand from the United States to Asia, provide incentives for transferring resources between tradable and non-tradable sectors, and improve the quality of growth from a social and environmental perspective.

The medium-term challenge — which will dominate the coming months and years — is to *shift from crisis response to structural policies* for growth. This essential, complicated manoeuvre will require both negative and positive actions. Emergency measures will need to be unwound, but to maintain the recovery, new, structural policies will need to be introduced to promote growth. Among structural measures, those that can generate early gains in employment will need to receive priority.

Importantly, the transition will require coherent policy actions across economies. For example, the withdrawal of the U.S. stimulus needs to be matched by continuing expansion in surplus economies to sustain global demand. Similarly, changes in monetary policy should be coordinated with policy changes in other regions in order to account for spillover effects and to minimize exchange rate and financial instability.

Reasons for Confidence

Despite these complexities, there is reason to hope that the transition to structural policies will be managed successfully. Today's policy challenges have been more intensely studied and are arguably better understood than any other economic problem in history. The G-20 has focused high-level attention on coherent global policies. The macroeconomic and financial fundamentals of many economies, especially in Asia, are strong. Asia's microeconomic fundamentals — entrepreneurial markets, robust innovation, and ample savings — have never been stronger.

Economies are also converging on key social priorities. These will help to resolve tensions that emerged in recent years: imbalances between North American and Asian net savings, between investment and consumption, between the production of public and private goods, between environmental quality and economic development, and among the incomes of different regions and population groups. These problems cannot be solved quickly, but there is more interest in finding solutions now than at any time in recent decades.

IBS growth does not require a significant — or possibly any — slowdown in the rate of growth. Evaluated by measures that account for externalities in production and welfare, the rate of growth could even accelerate. Deep recessions, such as the one the world has just experienced, tend to generate permanent losses in potential output, but they do not necessarily lower potential growth rates. Structural reforms and engines of growth associated with rebalancing can lead to new profit opportunities and spurts of innovation. This study argues that concerted Asia-Pacific initiatives can point governments and investors in directions that will sustain the recovery.

Reasons for Vigilance

Yet major risks also lie ahead. Foremost is the politics of economic policy in difficult times. Pressures for intervention will tempt officials to follow the "siren song" of short-term relief at the cost of medium-term growth. These pressures will mount as the pain caused by the crisis, including unemployment, persists well into the recovery. The list of false solutions ranges from unrestrained spending and lending to overregulation and trade protectionism.

Other risks arise from inherent economic uncertainties. The 2008–09 shock is the world's largest in eighty years, and the time needed to repair the damage from such shocks to balance sheets and investor confidence is historically measured in years, not months. For some time, consumers and investors will remain cautious, financial institutions fragile, and markets volatile. Confidence could deteriorate again before the recovery is complete. And unrelated problems, from natural disasters and disease to political events, could also overwhelm the recovery. Of course, these possibilities do not change the need for purposeful action.

A final risk is posed by policy conflicts among economies, such as tensions over trade, or inconsistencies in fiscal, monetary or regulatory approaches. The G-20 provides welcome leadership and envisions building a new framework for coherent global decisions. The WTO and the World Bank have made major contributions by publicizing protectionist measures, and the IMF and ADB have provided timely analysis and support for economies in trouble. So far, the world has avoided the disastrous policy anarchy of the 1930s. But much stronger cooperation is needed today to address the challenges that interdependence poses and to effect change in a setting no longer dominated by one or even a few countries.

III. CRISIS AND RECOVERY: A DRAMA IN PROGRESS

The events of 2007–2009 were not supposed to happen: the world economy was thrust into its deepest crisis in a century by the failure of its largest and arguably most sophisticated financial system. An effort to build a sustainable post-crisis economy must begin with understanding the origins and propagation of the crisis, the interventions that followed, and its consequences for the future of the Asia-Pacific.

The antecedents of the crisis can be traced back at least to the Asian financial crisis of 1997–98 and the collapse of the Internet bubble in the United States in 2000. A combination of conditions that started to emerge then — in the United States, highly accommodative monetary policies, powerful incentives for home ownership and lax financial regulation, and worldwide, a wave of financial innovation and strong demand for dollar assets — led over the following years to a large, wide-ranging buildup of leverage by households and financial firms in the United States and some other economies.

When interest rates rose and some asset prices began to decline in 2007, the leverage took its toll. The first cracks appeared with the failure of U.S. firms that issued sub-prime mortgages and/or held securities built from them. These complex, unregulated, poorly-understood instruments attracted many investors reaching for high yield. The crisis simmered for months as markets learned about the true extent of exposure to these and other weak assets, and about interconnections among giant financial firms. In September 2008, the collapse of Lehman Brothers, a large U.S. investment bank established in 1850, delivered the *coup de grâce* to financial markets. Contagion spread swiftly across asset classes, institutions and borders. A precipitous fall in trade and production soon followed. Towards the end of 2008, the state of the world economy was widely described as "Great Depression II".

A second great depression did not happen, but the crisis intensified with chilling speed. Its complexion changed markedly over time, unfolding as a drama in five distinct acts so far. Once the crisis became acute in the United States in September 2008, it engulfed the world, and some Asian economies became its worst casualties. But to the surprise of most forecasters the decline eased in mid-2009, and projections began to map a return to growth (Figure 1.1). The last act of the drama — recovery — is incomplete; much still depends on how policies are refocused on sustaining growth.

Act I: Decoupling?

Early in the crisis it appeared that Asia might be spared the worst. The recession in the United States began in December 2007, but growth in the

FIGURE 1.1
Deep V? Asia-Pacific GDP Growth Projections, 2007–2014

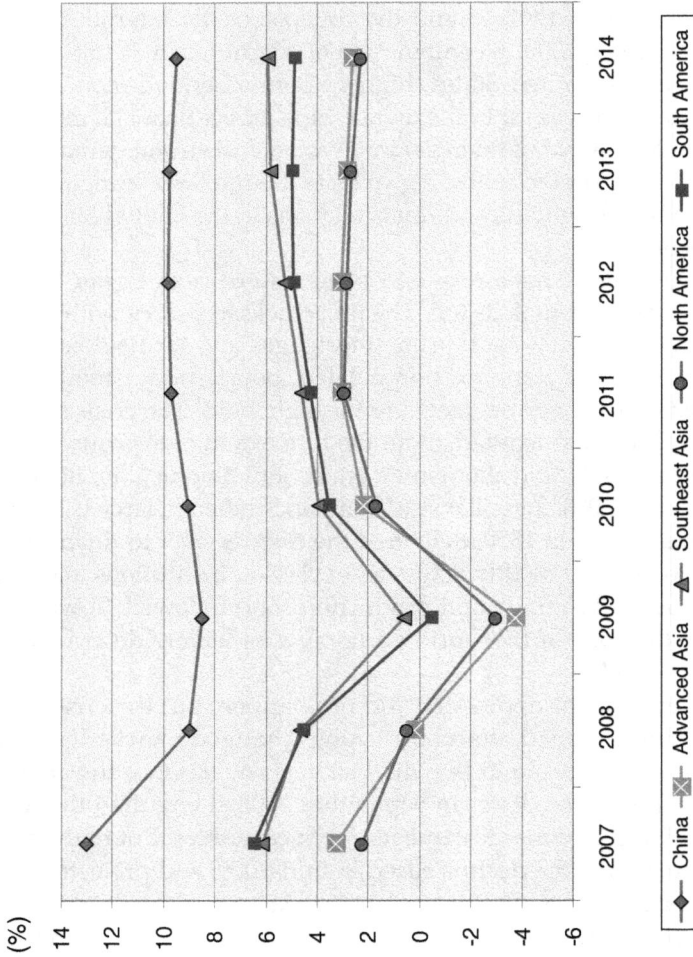

Source: IMF WEO (October 2009).

rest of the Asia-Pacific region remained positive for several months. The principal concern of most economies in the middle of 2008 was inflation, especially in oil and agricultural prices, and many ran monetary policy with a "foot on the brake". Until late 2008, Asian financial institutions largely escaped the problems plaguing U.S. and European banks. Chastened by the Asian financial crisis a decade earlier, Asian banks and regulators had maintained tighter reign on leverage and avoided many of the speculative investments that decimated U.S. and European balance sheets.

These developments led to the hypothesis that Asia's economy had "decoupled" from North America. Of course, few would have argued that complete decoupling was possible, given close trade and financial ties. Asia's intra-regional trade had increased rapidly over the previous decade, but much of this trade reflected the fragmentation of production within Asia and not a redirection of ultimate final demand. A majority of Asian manufactured exports still ended up, directly or indirectly as components, in goods sold in North America. Nevertheless, Asia's stable finances and microeconomic dynamism offered hope that the region could ride out the U.S. recession by replacing U.S. demand with regional and European sales.

Act II: Freefall

But U.S. and European imports did not merely slow, they swiftly collapsed. As sales plummeted, exporters halted purchases of intermediate inputs. For a while, economies engaged in assembly operations saw larger declines in imports (based on falling expectations) than in exports (based on past orders). The fragmentation of production into small steps carried out in several economies — a key innovation in manufacturing in recent decades — apparently speeded up and amplified the propagation of the trade shock. Sensitive "stocking decisions" appear to be an important characteristic of complex supply chains; in the downturn, de-stocking led to unexpected decline in demand, and in late 2009, re-stocking appears to be helping the recovery.

The effects of the crisis in the Asia-Pacific are summarized in Figure 1.2. Growth decelerated across the region by an average of 6 percentage points between 2007 and 2009 (Figure 1.2, Panel A). A handful of economies, including Japan, Singapore, Chinese Taipei and others we classify as Advanced Asia, experienced much steeper declines due to their product

Yongfu Cao et al.

FIGURE 1.2
Dimensions of the Crisis: No Place to Hide

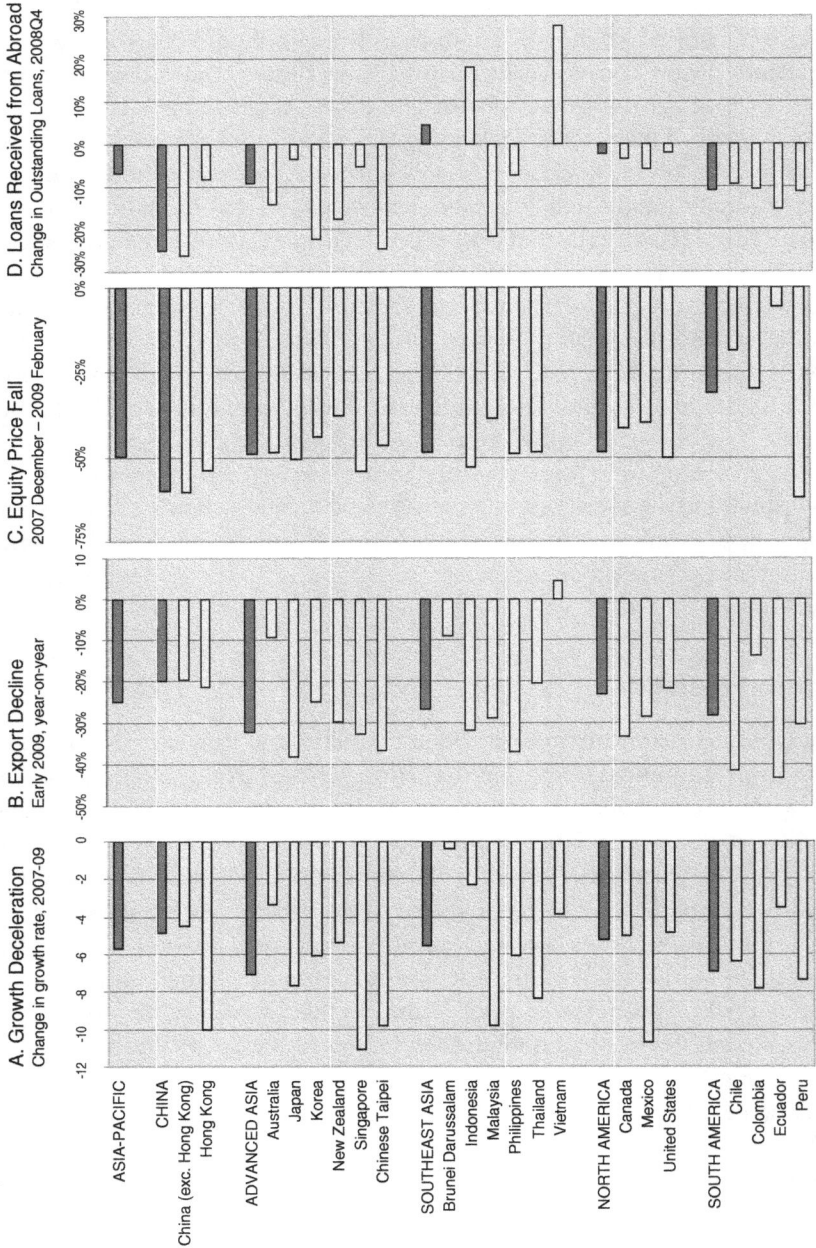

Sources: BIS, CEIC, Yahoo Finance.

mix. The impact also varied with the initial growth rates of economies — for example, China grew at nearly 13 per cent in 2007, so even a 5 per cent decline left it with an enviable 8 per cent growth rate.

Trade collapsed (Figure 1.2, Panel B) broadly, and especially so in certain subgroups of manufactured products. American consumers sharply reduced purchases of luxury goods such as autos, sophisticated electronics, and communications equipment. (Durables and luxuries are cyclical since households typically adjust these expenditures first.) Declining sales were amplified by the efforts of retailers and importers to reduce inventory. This generated declines in orders for sophisticated products and components, produced mainly by advanced Asian exporters such as Japan, Korea and Singapore, and by Mexico.

Financial markets also served to transmit the downturn. Equity markets fell by roughly one-half between December 2007, when markets were near their recent highs, and February 2009, when most appear to have reached lows (Figure 1.2, Panel C). The crash was similar everywhere — the declines were only slightly larger in riskier markets such as China and Southeast Asia, and only slightly smaller in relatively sheltered markets such as New Zealand. As a result, wealth declined and economic forecasts turned sharply negative. These in turn took their toll on consumption and investment.

The downturn was further amplified by retrenchment in international lending. In late 2008, banks curtailed their international lending to consolidate capital positions at home (Figure 1.2, Panel D). For example, the Korean won fell sharply due to concerns about foreign currency debt, despite reasonable economic fundamentals. Several economies even experienced difficulties in accessing trade credit to maintain exports. Fortunately, the constraints on trade credit eased relatively quickly as markets improved and development banks and other institutions jumped in to provide targeted funding for trade.

The propagation of the crisis through the Asia-Pacific region is illustrated in Figure 1.3 with reference to the evolution of GDP in four economies.

- *United States.* U.S. consumption began to decline in late 2007 with the sub-prime mortgage collapse and falling house prices. Investment contributions were stable in 2007 but became quite negative as the downturn gained momentum. Government expenditures contributed

Yongfu Cao et al.

FIGURE 1.3
How the Crisis Spread from the United States to Asia

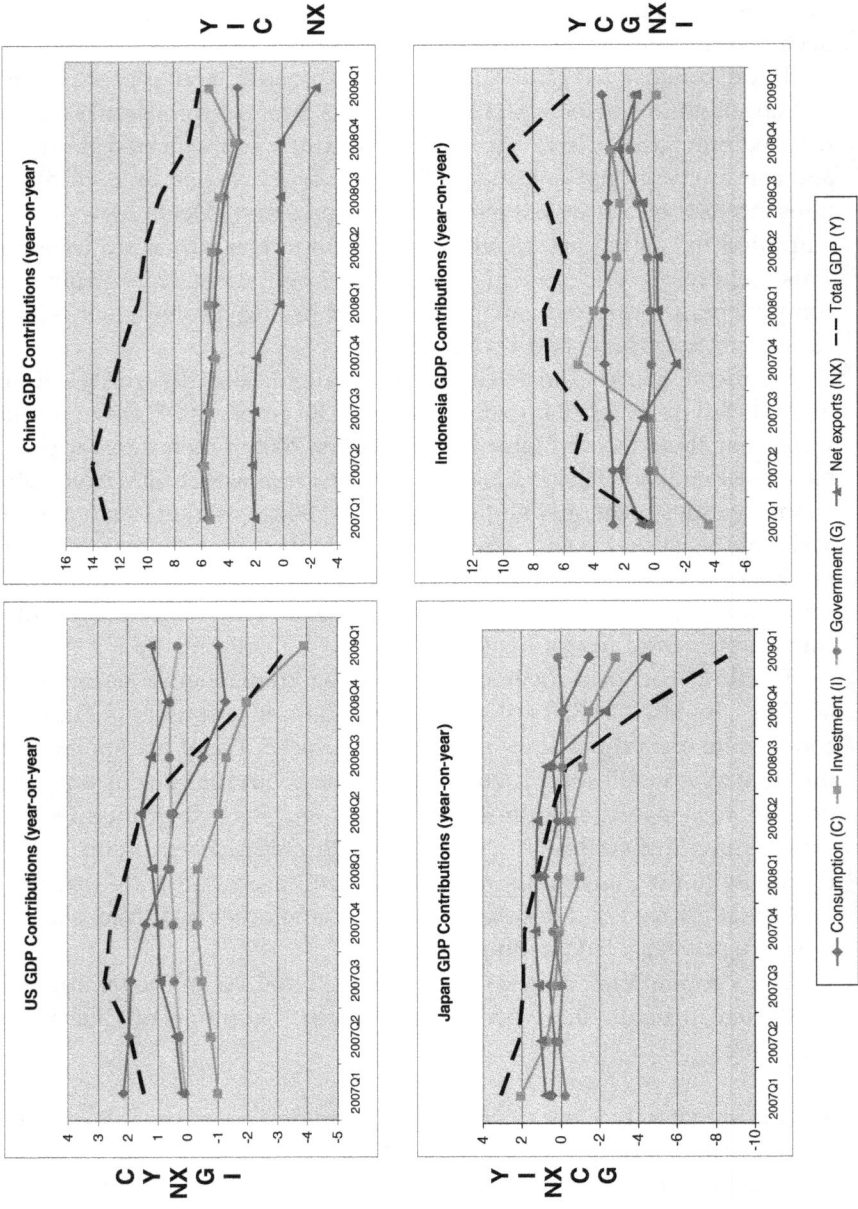

Source: Calculations based on CEIC data.

positively, but by a small margin, as state government cutbacks offset the impact of federal stabilizers. Net exports were also positive, as imports fell sharply, transmitting the crisis to other Asia-Pacific economies.

- *Japan*. Consumption, government spending and net exports held up through much of 2008. But investment was slowing, perhaps anticipating a downturn, and the economy began to contract in 2008Q2. Then, as in other Advanced Asian exporters and Mexico, net exports fell very sharply in 2008Q4, reflecting falling U.S. demand. The decline was later reinforced by "knock-on effects" in domestic investment and consumption.

- *China*. Like Japan, China experienced a slow decline in demand through 2008, leading to a moderating growth rate. But this was enough to elicit a strong policy response, and by the time the export shock hit China (it came later and was smaller than for Japan) measures had been introduced to support investment. Consumption remained flat and investment rose in 2009Q1, moderating the decline.

- *Indonesia*. As some other ASEAN and Latin American economies, Indonesia survived the crisis relatively well. Its GDP components increased somewhat in 2008 (in some cases benefiting from rising primary goods prices), and the growth rate rose. The export shock hit in 2009Q1, but represented a smaller share of GDP and was partly offset by consumption. Growth slowed but stayed positive.

In short, powerful transmission mechanisms — operating through trade, financial markets, and financial flows — led to similar impacts in many economies, even those with the strongest fundamentals. Differences in effects were mostly due to differences in specialization: economies producing advanced, durable goods fared worst. Some differences in the recovery were related to the speed and scale of policy reactions, and larger economies had more freedom to act. But on the whole, the crisis left "no place to hide". No policy could have insulated an economy from it, aside from the highly unattractive option of restricting specialization and trade. But exposures were amplified by high exports associated with current account surpluses.

Act III: Governments to the Rescue

The policy reactions of the Asia-Pacific region have been as remarkable as the crisis itself. Monetary easing began in the United States in 2007, but emergency financial operations in the United States and Europe dramatically intensified in the fall of 2008. Reactions in Asia and Latin America were more muted, since Asian financial firms were less exposed to "toxic assets". (More detailed assessments are provided in the subsequent sub-regional chapters.)

Monetary and financial measures included very low policy interest rates; central bank purchases of securities in asset classes such as long-term bonds, corporate securities and mortgage pools; wide-ranging guarantees of financial institutions and money-market mutual funds;[1] effective nationalization and government-managed mergers of vulnerable financial institutions; and lending against impaired assets. Between September and November 2008, the Federal Reserve System of the United States more than doubled its balance sheet and radically altered the composition of its assets from short-term government securities to a wide range of assets. The Bank of England took similar steps; the European Central Bank and the Bank of Japan also reacted.

Monetary easing was accompanied by large fiscal measures. Altogether, Asia-Pacific economies adopted stimulus packages of US$1.7 trillion, or 84 per cent of the total worldwide discretionary stimulus, as estimated by Khatiwada (2009). China announced a RMB4 trillion stimulus package (US$586 billion) on 9 November 2008, less than two months after the Lehman Brothers collapse, and the United States adopted the US$787 billion American Recovery and Reinvestment Act on 17 February 2009.[2] Japan, despite high debt levels, mounted several packages. Significant packages were also adopted in Malaysia, Singapore, Mexico and other Asia-Pacific economies. European stimulus programmes were not launched until later, although somewhat stronger stabilizers in Europe reacted to the crisis automatically as it deepened.

Policy responses in the Asia-Pacific area are summarized in Figure 1.4. The announced fiscal policy packages are shown in Panel A (the package totals include expenditures planned for future years), while the actual deterioration in government balances in 2009 is shown in Panel B. Monetary policy is tracked in the next two panels. As Panel C shows that Japan, the United States and Korea forced policy rates to near zero, and Panel D indicates that all economies reduced policy rates by significant margins.

The smaller regional economies faced difficult choices. Most entered the crisis with strong fiscal balances and financial institutions, yet their thinly traded currencies, small financial markets and relatively open current

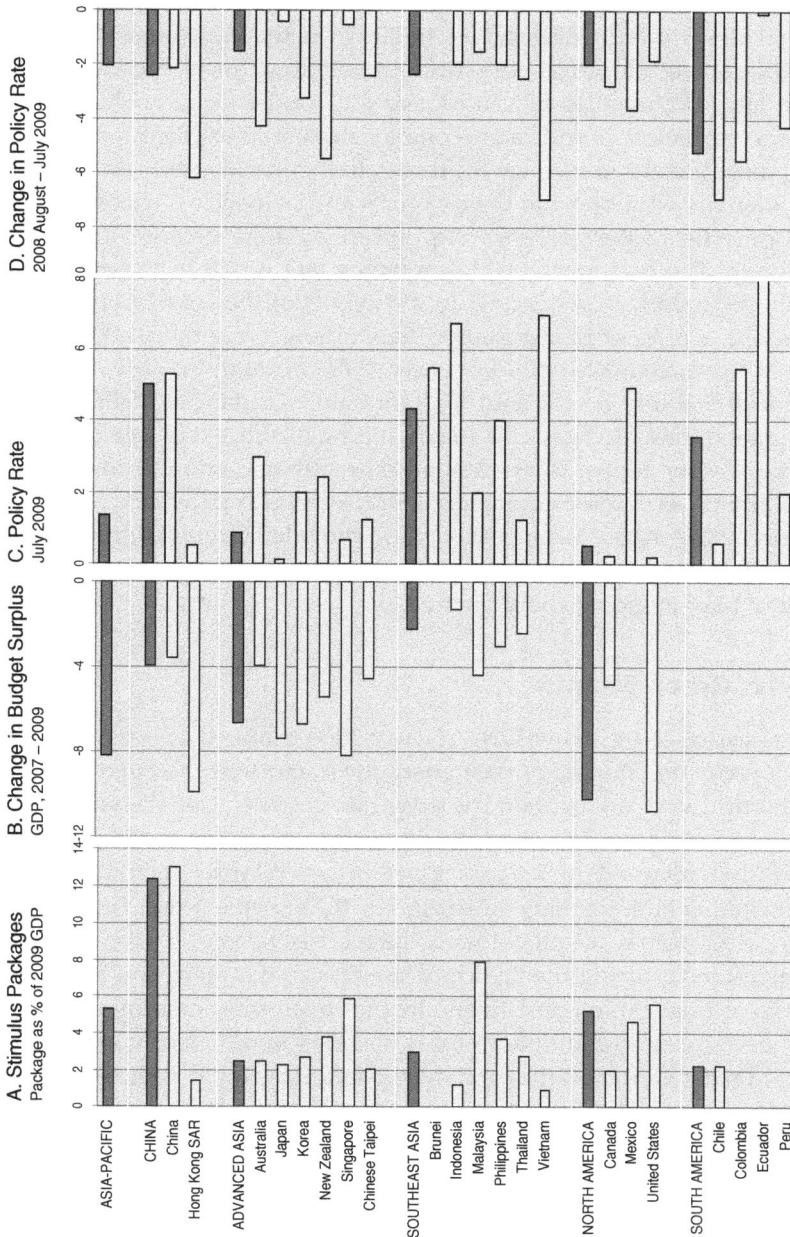

FIGURE 1.4
Policy: Massive Responses across the Region

A. Stimulus Packages
Package as % of 2009 GDP

B. Change in Budget Surplus
GDP, 2007 – 2009

C. Policy Rate
July 2009

D. Change in Policy Rate
2008 August – July 2009

Sources: Khatiwada (2009), AEM (June 2009), CEIC.

accounts left them vulnerable. If they failed to act, or acted too aggressively, capital flows would undermine stability. In the end, most managed a middle course, adopting some stimulus and accepting some depreciation. Even larger economies like Indonesia and Korea faced challenges from currency speculation, and had to combine market adjustments with bilateral swap negotiations to manage the threat. In the end, depreciated currencies provided an extra boost to their exports and helped to support growth.

Domestic responses were supported by high-profile international meetings. The leaders of G-20 economies met on 15 November 2008 in Washington and — in contrast to the events of the Great Depression — launched a process of vigorous collaboration. Over the next year, they agreed to issue US$250 billion in new SDRs through the IMF; turned the Financial Stability Forum into the more global Financial Stability Board; designated the G-20 summit as a continuing forum; established a detailed work plan[3] for cooperation on financial regulation and macroeconomics; and committed to reforming votes in the IMF and World Bank. In addition, important international support was also provided through ad hoc currency swap arrangements. More remains to be done, but the crisis has raised the state of play in global cooperation.

Act IV: Green Shoots

The severity of the downturn in early 2009 dimmed expectations for a quick recovery. Studies of past crises indicated that the events of 2007–2009 followed an especially adverse course: the downturn was synchronized across the world and included a wide-ranging financial crisis that resulted in a large asset price collapse and substantially weakened major financial institutions (Claessens, Kose and Terrones 2009). Recovery is usually slow in such crises because of the challenges involved in restoring the health of the financial system and the balance sheets of households and firms. In the meantime, employment losses further depress economic activity. If the crisis is sufficiently long-lived, it can reduce potential output and even potential growth rates by removing factors of production or making them less effective. Thus, most forecasters envisioned at best a U-shaped recovery with a long period of slow growth. The most frequently downloaded paper on a popular policy website showed that the current crisis and the Great Depression were following highly similar trajectories (Eichengreen and O'Rourke 2009).

The first positive news came from China. The stimulus programme there, combining government spending with aggressive credit growth by partly state-owned banks, had a quick impact on economic activity. Falling exports had driven many export-oriented companies to the brink, and in 2009Q1 Chinese GDP slowed, to a still-respectable annual rate of 6.1 per cent. As the effects of policy began to take hold, Chinese investment expanded rapidly and activity picked up. In 2009Q2 China grew by 7.9 per cent and growth for 2009 eventually exceeded the 8 per cent target.

In the middle of 2009, the export decline generally stopped and some economies began to register a rebound (Figure 1.5, Panel B). Combined with aggressive stimulus, the stabilization of exports led to surprising quarter-to-quarter increases in output in 2009Q2 in Hong Kong, Japan, Singapore and other economies. The United States joined the "green shoots" camp soon after the government managed to restore confidence in financial markets in March 2009. Unexpected improvements in housing markets and construction soon followed, and returning confidence led to a sharp rise in equity prices (Figure 1.5, Panel C). In the six month from the February lows to the end of August 2009, markets recovered roughly half of the losses experienced from the 2007 highs. With growing confidence, net lending by banks abroad also stabilized in the middle of 2009, and indeed recovered at a brisk pace to borrowers in Advanced Asia (Figure 1.5, Panel D).

Act V: Recovery

The outlook brightened in the summer of 2009. The IMF, which had revised its projections for global economic growth progressively downward from April 2008 to April 2009, increased its estimates in July and October 2009 (IMF 2009). IMF projections for the Asia-Pacific region updated in October 2009 (Figure 1.5, Panel A) show growth rates over 2010–14 to be similar to those in 2007 and the years prior to the crisis. For Asia's emerging economies, the consensus converged on a V-shaped recovery.

The United States also resumed growth by the 2009Q3, and is expected to continue growing at a moderate pace in 2010. The only economy projected to have a significantly lower growth rate in the next five years than in 2007 is China — but it was growing unsustainably rapidly then (12.8 per cent). Southeast Asia and Latin America, as well as Australia and New Zealand, escaped the crisis with less damage than other sub-regions,

FIGURE 1.5
Recovery: Work in Progress

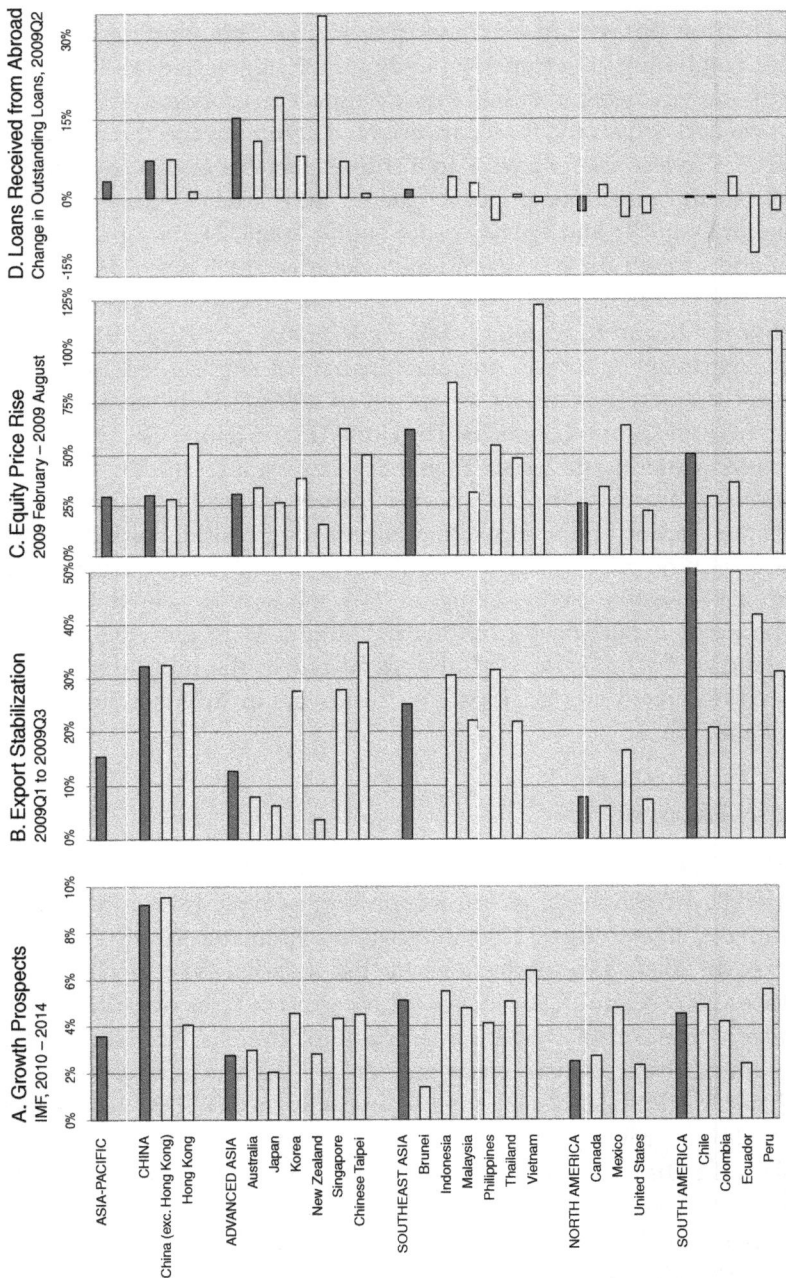

A. Growth Prospects
IMF, 2010 – 2014

B. Export Stabilization
2009Q1 to 2009Q3

C. Equity Price Rise
2009 February – 2009 August

D. Loans Received from Abroad
Change in Outstanding Loans, 2009Q2

Sources: IMF WEO (October 2009), CEIC, Yahoo Finance, BIS (December 2009).

and should recover relatively quickly. Early fears of a collapse in remittances did not come to pass, a factor that proved important for the Philippines, Mexico and South American economies.

But the recovery is not assured. Many forecasters expect anaemic progress, as investment and especially employment recover slowly in the United States. Others even foresee a second downturn. Adverse scenarios typically assume that China and the United States are not be able to transition to new models of growth by 2011 or 2012. In the United States, worries focus on government budget deficits, persistent unemployment and continued financial turmoil; in China the concerns relate to the heavy role of bank lending in stimulating investment, while household consumption continues to be too low.

Europe's contribution to world growth is projected to be modest in the near term. The European economy appears to be rebounding, but continuing consumer and investor caution, risks associated with exposure to sovereign debt in Eastern Europe and the heavily indebted members of the European Union, and the real appreciation of the euro point to sluggish economic activity. The IMF projects that Europe will recover more slowly than the United States. Thus, world growth in 2010 and 2011 will depend heavily on emerging markets.

Pessimistic scenarios incorporate some of the following elements:

- *Premature policy tightening.* Monetary or fiscal policies could be tightened too early, due to rising concerns about inflation, excessive growth in lending, or currency instability; or governments could encounter difficulties in financing deficits.
- *Insufficient private demand.* Private spending could remain depressed due to persistent unemployment, falling asset prices, uncertainty about growth, unrelated shocks (say, from disasters or disease) and, in the United States, high debt.
- *Persistent financial fragility.* Financial markets and intermediation could stay volatile due to slow progress in isolating bad assets, regulatory interventions that increase risk aversion, rising concerns about sovereign debt, or the renewal of imbalances that threaten stability.
- *Expanding imbalances.* The U.S. administration projects that the U.S. budget deficit will be reduced from well over 10 per cent of GDP in 2009 to 5.1 per cent in 2012. The spending cuts and tax increases needed to achieve this better outcome will face heavy opposition. Similarly, Chinese surpluses could climb. These developments could create new turmoil in currency and asset markets.

Individually or in combination, these factors would restrain growth throughout the Asia-Pacific. Most likely, they would be then amplified by declines in asset prices. And since governments have pushed policy options hard in the crisis, they have less ammunition left for another battle. Thus, while a reasonable path to recovery is feasible, as reflected in IMF projections, policy mistakes or other adverse developments could easily lead to much worse outcomes.

IV. STRATEGIES FOR SUSTAINED GROWTH

As the recovery proceeds, policy-makers face difficult decisions on exiting policies adopted at the height of the crisis and on building foundations for sustained post-crisis growth. The debate initially focused more on the former than the latter. Yet the two types of decisions are linked: the sooner structural policies for medium-term growth begin to work, the sooner stimulus packages can be discontinued. Indeed, the risk in exiting the stimulus programmes derives from not having effective structural initiatives in place. This section examines four types of structural measures:

- Demand-side measures to make spending sustainable in the principal expenditure categories of each economy.
- Supply-side measures to stimulate resources flows to and productivity growth in sectors neglected in the past.
- Initiatives to launch growth engines that generate new opportunities for investment, employment and output.
- Initiatives in international cooperation to generate global strategies and to help make national efforts consistent and effective.

We begin by reviewing structural threats to post-crisis growth and strategies to address them.

The Threat of Imbalances

Asia-Pacific growth prior to the crisis was spearheaded by consumption in the United States and to a lesser extent Europe. The exuberance of U.S. households spilled into U.S. current account deficits exceeding 6 per cent of U.S. GDP in 2006, financed by the accumulation of financial assets by China, Japan and other advanced Asian economies (see Figure 1.6). In

FIGURE 1.6
Imbalances Change Rapidly
(Current account, US$ billion)

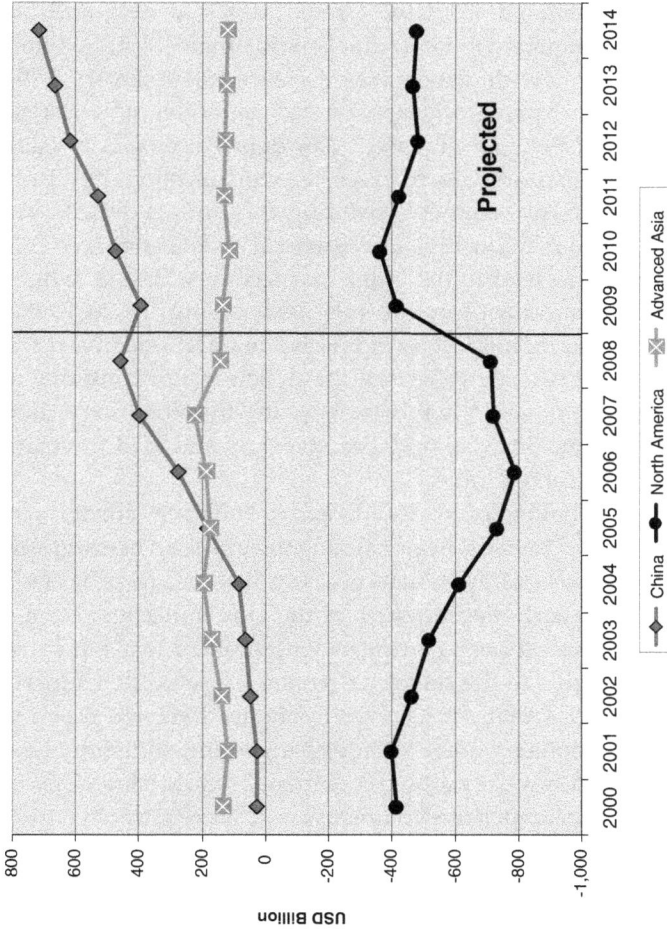

Source: IMF WEO Database, October 2009.

2009, the imbalances fell sharply, partly because U.S. consumers returned to more typical savings rates. But while the IMF expects U.S. current account deficits to remain stable in the near future, it expects China's surpluses to rise, leading to a sharp overall increase the Asia-Pacific's surplus with the world.[4]

Shifting demand from the United States to Asia and other surplus regions will require coherent, timely adjustments. If U.S. demand remains weak and no new demand takes its place, the recovery will stall. But if U.S. demand expands vigorously and generates new deficits, then the recovery will become unstable. The deficit scenario remains a serious concern, not so much due to excessive consumption, but due to the rapid increase of U.S. government spending and budget deficits. While there is no mechanical relationship between fiscal and current account deficits, the former tends to lead to the latter in a recovery, that is, when investment and consumption activity are relatively strong. In 2009, the U.S. fiscal deficit reached its highest level relative to GDP since World War II. If the government is unable to reduce the deficit rapidly, internal and external debt will rise, raising the prospects of inflation and instability. Sooner or later, these concerns will unnerve investors and lead to volatility in asset prices and exchange rates.

Forward-looking markets will tend to "balance" current accounts (even without policy changes) by penalizing the build-up of *ex ante* unsustainable imbalances. For example, markets may respond to projected imbalances with a sharp, early depreciation of the U.S. dollar and/or a sharp, early increase in interest rates on dollar-denominated loans. If some currencies are fixed relative to the dollar, as is the case with the Chinese RMB, then other currencies that can change freely are likely to move with greater amplitude, imposing greater trade changes and adjustment costs on those economies. In any case, the adjustments would slow U.S. spending by making it more expensive to borrow and more attractive to save, and by increasing the real cost of tradable products to U.S. consumers. Similar mechanisms would work in the opposite direction in surplus economies, unless they act to contain excessive savings.

But automatic feedback mechanisms would limit imbalances at the possibly high cost of exchange rate and asset price turmoil. If sustainability is left entirely to market adjustments, large and uneven price changes might result, due to uncertainty about policy and other factors. When imbalances rise, market participants cannot immediately tell whether this is due to excessive spending or other, transient factors. Markets could therefore permit imbalances to escalate until the forces driving them are clear — and much larger adjustments are needed. Whether or not such cycles develop, unsustainable policies increase uncertainty and diminish the efficiency of investment and consumption decisions.

This pattern of market corrections to imbalances imposes costly stop-and-go patterns on the real economy. For example, in the pre-crisis period, export industries thrived in Asia and languished in the United States. As markets reacted, exports shrank in Asia and incentives improved for tradables in the United States. Such shifts impose permanent costs in both economies because they require capacity to be shut down in some industries and new capacity to be created in others. Capital, skills, knowledge and productivity are lost in declining sectors, and have to be built up anew in the expanding sectors.

For all of these reasons, policies that balance expenditures within and across economies are necessary to ensure stable growth. The relationship between global recovery and global imbalances is illustrated in Figure 1.7. Here the growth rate of the world economy is used as a proxy for recovery, and the U.S. current account deficit as a proxy for imbalances. The diagram indicates four possible outcomes, ranging from a worst scenario with a low world growth rate and high U.S. deficits (quadrant C) to the best scenario with a high world growth rate and low U.S. deficits (quadrant B).

Prior to the crisis, global growth was adequate, but U.S. deficits were large (as illustrated by the pre-crisis point in quadrant D). During the crisis, the world economy moved to unacceptably low growth, but deficits shrank to an acceptable level (the post-crisis point in quadrant A). With recovery, the global economy is now moving along the solid arrow towards higher growth and larger deficits. But the future is uncertain, as represented in the diagram by three alternative dashed arrows. The eventual path of the world economy could approach balanced growth (ending up in quadrant B), but it could also lead to undesirable outcomes with unsustainable capital flows and/or low growth rates.

The IMF projections envision a sustainable growth path, as illustrated in Figure 1.8. The IMF expects world growth to return to near 4 per cent (above the 3.1 per cent average for the 1997–2007 decade) and U.S. deficits to remain under 3 per cent, an arbitrary but widely used target for sustainability. The IMF trajectory reflects a relatively sluggish recovery of

FIGURE 1.7
The Recovery Needs to be Sustainable

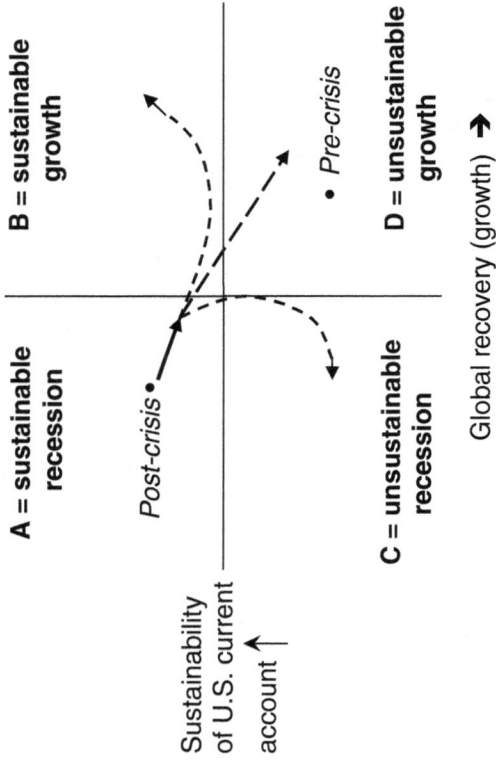

A = sustainable recession

B = sustainable growth

C = unsustainable recession

D = unsustainable growth

Post-crisis •

• Pre-crisis

Sustainability of U.S. current account

Global recovery (growth)

FIGURE 1.8
Some Projections Envision Balanced Recovery, Some Not

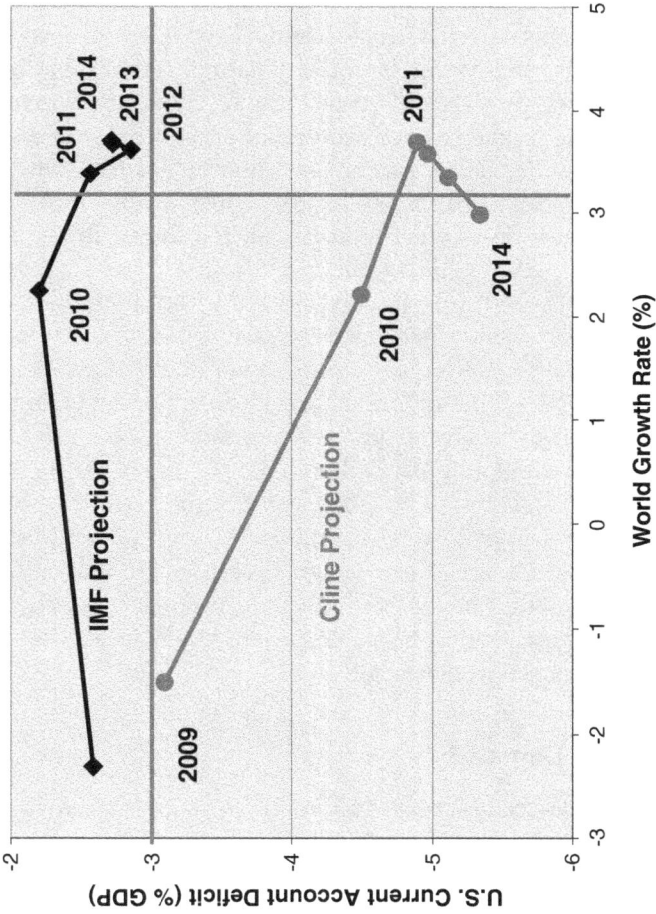

Source: IMF WEO (October 2009), Cline (2009).

U.S. consumer spending and investment, and steady unwinding of the fiscal stimulus.

In the medium term, while the U.S. dollar remains the world's principal reserve currency, the United States is likely to run a current account deficit, or equivalently, other economies are likely to accumulate dollar assets. The 3 per cent target rate corresponds, roughly, to the potential long-term growth rate of the U.S. economy. Even if U.S. external debt were to expand at this rate forever, it would eventually stabilize at 100 per cent of GDP. The rate is probably best viewed as acceptable only in the medium term, facilitating global reserve accumulation and measured adjustment in both surplus and deficit economies. The rate is consistent with larger surplus percentages in other, smaller economies. For example, if the 3 per cent U.S. capital inflows were to come entirely from China, they would represent 8 per cent of Chinese GDP.

Some forecasts of future imbalances are less optimistic than those of the IMF. William Cline (2009) projects lower world growth rates and higher imbalances; he sees U.S. current account deficits growing to 4.9 per cent of U.S. GDP by 2011 and remaining close to that level thereafter. In a still more adverse scenario, Cline assumes larger budget deficits, which push the U.S. current account deficit to 5.2 per cent GDP by 2015 and to 16 per cent of GDP by 2030. Cline incorporates two plausible — but hopefully too pessimistic — assumptions: that the U.S. will fail to reduce government deficits, and that foreign investors (especially China) will continue to demand U.S. assets with only modest increases in interest rates. Due to these assumptions, neither of Cline's scenarios enters the desirable quadrant B in Figure 1.8.

Rebalancing Demand

To reduce net external surpluses and deficits of an economy, adjustments are needed: (i) in the overall level of demand and (ii) in the composition of demand between tradable and non-tradable sectors. In the United States, the deficit economy, rebalancing the current account requires a reduction in overall demand relative to income, and a shift in demand from non-tradables to tradables. In surplus Asia, rebalancing requires an increase in overall demand and a shift in demand from tradables to non-tradables (especially services).

Shifts in an economy's domestic demand may result from changes in consumption or investment (and hence deeper determinants such as wealth, taxes, and credit and business conditions) or from policy changes that affect government spending. Shifts in the composition of demand typically reflect price changes, and specifically movements in the real exchange rate.[5] For example, the currencies of deficit economies can be expected to depreciate in the process of rebalancing, because declining domestic demand will reduce the prices of the economy's non-traded goods and drive resources into industries that serve external (export) demand.

Flexible exchange rates normally facilitate the currency adjustments required to achieve expenditure switching and rebalancing. But since China and some other economies manage their exchange rates, these adjustments also require policy decisions. After appreciating by 17 per cent in nominal terms against the dollar between 2005 and 2008, the Chinese RMB has remained constant relative to the dollar through 2009. Since the dollar depreciated against other currencies in 2009, this has also meant that the RMB has depreciated in trade-weighted terms, particularly against the Japanese yen. In effect, the RMB has moved in a direction opposite to that required for expenditure switching.

Future adjustments will require renewed flexibility against the U.S. dollar. Of course, exchange rate changes cannot work except as part of a package of policy measures that drive the necessary expenditure shifts. Moreover, given the Asia-Pacific's complex, fragmented production system, several currencies would have to move against the dollar (BIS 2009) in order to change the overall price of goods exported to the United States. These complicate policy and argue for greater regional cooperation in policy changes. But decisions about real exchange rates cannot be avoided. In the absence of flexibility in nominal exchange rates, market mechanisms may result in more costly adjustments in real exchange rates, namely through price level changes that involve deflation in deficit economies and inflation in surplus economies.

To provide insight into the magnitudes involved in rebalancing, Table 1.1 presents an overview of expenditures and imbalances in the Asia-Pacific region in 2007, the last "normal" year before the crisis. The largest current account imbalances in the region consisted of the U.S. deficit of US$727 billion and China's surplus of US$372 billion. Other important surplus economies included Japan and other Advanced Asian economies; other deficit economies include Australia and New Zealand. Overall, the region ran a deficit of US$127 billion with the rest of the world. Europe had a slight current account surplus (netting out substantial surpluses and deficits), while the Middle East and the Rest of the World had

TABLE 1.1
Pre-crisis Expenditures Were Not Sustainable
(2007 Data, US$ billion)

	GDP	Expenditures						Current Acct
		Cons	Inv	Gov	Exp	Imp	Net Exp	
World	**54,841**	**31,835**	**12,810**	**9,810**	**17,149**	**16,763**	**386**	**299**
European Union (EU15)	15,724	8,998	3,359	3,227	6,147	6,006	141	9
Middle East	1,394	589	347	203	811	556	255	265
Rest of the World	8,895	4,742	2,575	1,462	3,076	2,959	117	63
Asia–Pacific	**28,827**	**17,506**	**6,529**	**4,919**	**7,115**	**7,242**	**–127**	**–38**
China	**3,652**	**1,340**	**1,493**	**488**	**1,773**	**1,443**	**330**	**397**
China (exc. Hong Kong)	3,445	1,216	1,450	472	1,342	1,035	308	372
Hong Kong	207	125	43	17	431	408	22	26
Advanced Asia	**7,028**	**3,915**	**1,772**	**1,188**	**2,100**	**1,947**	**153**	**221**
Australia	910	508	257	161	183	199	–17	–57
Japan	4,384	2,469	1,057	786	772	699	73	211
Korea	1,049	571	309	154	440	424	16	6
New Zealand	131	76	32	25	38	39	–1	–11
Singapore	168	64	35	16	384	332	53	39
Chinese Taipei	385	227	83	47	283	254	29	33
Southeast Asia	**1,089**	**640**	**268**	**111**	**637**	**567**	**70**	**60**
Brunei Darussalam	12	2	2	3	8	3	5	6
Indonesia	436	275	108	36	127	110	17	10
Malaysia	187	85	41	23	206	168	38	29
Philippines	137	100	22	14	62	61	1	7
Thailand	247	132	66	31	180	161	19	14
Vietnam	70	46	30	4	55	64	–10	–7
North America	**16,533**	**11,294**	**2,880**	**3,060**	**2,446**	**3,147**	**–701**	**–720**
Canada	1,432	799	326	279	500	471	29	15
Mexico	1,023	669	266	105	290	306	–17	–8
United States	14,078	9,826	2,289	2,676	1,656	2,370	–714	–727
South America	**525**	**316**	**117**	**71**	**160**	**138**	**21**	**4**
Chile	164	89	34	18	77	55	23	7
Colombia	208	132	51	34	35	44	–9	–6
Ecuador	46	29	11	5	16	16	0	2
Peru	107	66	21	13	31	24	7	1

surpluses, as did the world as a whole (due to statistical inconsistencies). The table also shows significant differences in the pattern of expenditures; while the United States produced 49 per cent of the Asia-Pacific's GDP, it accounted for 56 per cent of the area's consumption and only 35 per cent of its investment.

What would it have taken to eliminate excessive imbalances in the Asia-Pacific in 2007? A hypothetical recalculation of Table 1.1 can help to assess the scale of the adjustments that might be required. We anchor this scenario by assuming that the United States deficit is reduced to 3 per cent of GDP (US$422 billion), or by US$304 billion, for reasons explained above. The scenario requires further assumptions on how adjustments are distributed across other economies and how they are allocated to expenditures within them.

A second set of assumptions involves the allocation of the US$304 billion reduction in the U.S. deficit to other economies with current account surpluses. This was accomplished by allocating the reduction to each surplus economy in proportion to its share of the sum of all global surpluses in 2007. This implies, for example, that China would absorb 33 per cent of the U.S. deficit reduction, reducing its surplus by US$102 billion. (This allocation is simple but essentially arbitrary — for example, a case could be made for alternative approaches that allocate more- or less-than-proportional reductions to other economies such as Japan and the Middle East.)

A third set of assumptions involves the allocation of changes in overall national expenditures within each economy to specific expenditure categories. This was based on country-specific assumptions that commonly appear in discussions of rebalancing. For example, overall 60 per cent of the expenditure adjustments were allocated to consumption in the United States and China (where consumption rates are widely considered to be too high and too low, respectively) and to investment in Southeast Asia (where investment rates are considered too low, especially compared to levels achieved before 1997–98). In all cases, 20 per cent of adjustment was allocated to each of the other two expenditure categories.

The goal of the exercise is to offer insight into the size of adjustments associated with eliminating the excess imbalances of 2007 (Figure 1.9). In China, for example, the recalculation implies consumption 5 per cent above its actual 2007 level. This is equivalent to the growth in consumption that normally takes place in eight months given China's rapid development.

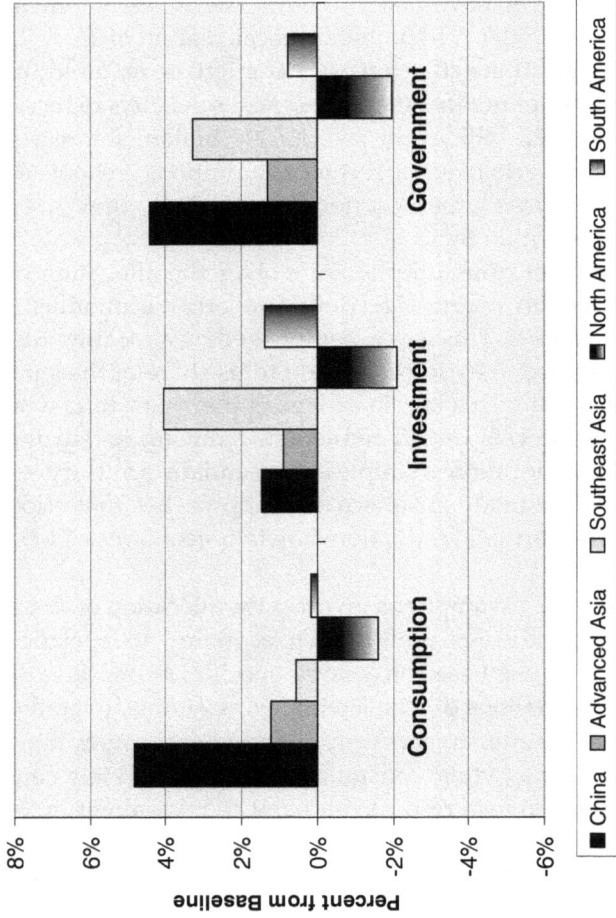

FIGURE 1.9
Rebalancing Requires Moderate Expenditure Changes
(% change from 2007 baseline)

Source: Calculations explained in text.

Put another way, China's consumption growth would have to exceed the rate of growth of GDP by 1.67 per cent per year over a three year period (say, it would have to grow at a nominal rate of 11.7 per cent per year rather than 10 per cent per year). It is a matter of judgement, of course, whether such acceleration is considered "small" or "large", since significant policy measures have to be taken. But a detailed study of consumption-increasing policies by the McKinsey Global Institute suggests that with the right initiatives even greater increases in consumption could be achieved (Woetzel et al. 2009).

Similar percentage changes would be involved in investment and government expenditures in Southeast Asia and South America. The demand effects in the United States would be smaller, amounting to around 2 per cent reductions in various U.S. expenditures. The scale of these results suggests that the adjustments are manageable — and indeed considerably smaller than some market-driven changes that have taken place in recent months.

Figure 1.10 reports the trade impacts of these same recalculations. This requires a fourth set of assumptions, in which we allocate half of the change in the net exports to exports, and half to imports. This would lead to around 5 per cent change in U.S. trade (including a larger increase in exports, and a smaller decrease in imports), and around 2–4 per cent changes in trade in other sub-regions. Given relatively modest expenditure changes, it is not surprising that other studies find that the sectoral impacts of rebalancing are also manageable (Kawai and Zhai 2009 and Petri 2009). Thus, the arithmetic of rebalancing is generally favourable: imbalances that exert great stress on global financial relations are relatively small when compared to broad classes of domestic expenditures within large economies. Shifting expenditures, although politically difficult, will likely cause relatively small structural dislocations within the region's economies.

Nevertheless, quantitatively modest adjustments may involve deep policy changes and significant political effort. The details of these policies are discussed in the sub-regional essays. For example, increasing consumption in China is likely to require a redistribution of income from the corporate sector to households, as well as improvements in social safety nets. These changes would require substantial improvements in the operation of factor markets — labour and capital markets — that enable workers to command higher wages that are more closely aligned with their productivity, and give small firms better access to finance. And those

FIGURE 1.10
Rebalancing Requires Moderate Trade Changes
(% change from 2007 baseline)

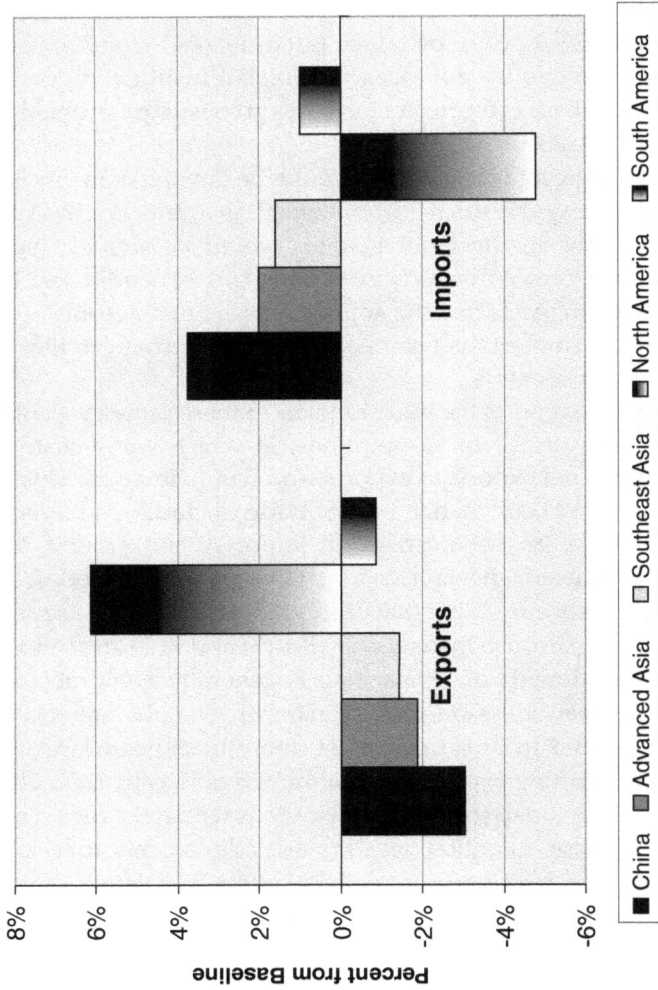

Source: Calculations explained in text.

changes, in turn, might require adjustments in the incentive systems used within the government bureaucracy.

Similarly, a balanced growth path will require difficult political decisions in the United States. The U.S. current account deficit has declined to around 3 per cent of GDP in 2009, due to a remarkable increase in net private savings to 10 per cent of GDP, which in turn reflects declines in investment and consumption spending. But the U.S. government budget deficit, already large before the crisis due to tax cuts and military expenditures, has risen dramatically. Many new priorities, such as expanded health insurance coverage, have also emerged with the change in administrations in 2009. The U.S. budget deficit is now at levels not seen since World War II. Although there is no one-to-one relationship between the fiscal and external deficits, the two are likely to move together once U.S. investment recovers. Massive fiscal consolidation would then be needed to keep U.S. external balances stable, possibly in the context of high unemployment. Solutions are likely to require major political changes; for example, Bergsten (2009) proposes that the United States add a "balanced budget amendment" to its constitution.

Rebalancing Supply

If demand patterns change, supply patterns will also need to adjust, requiring resource movements between tradable and non-tradable production. In the United States, where rebalancing will require increased net exports, resources will need to move from non-tradable sectors into tradable ones. Such transfers require price signals, which typically reflect exchange rate adjustments.

In the years before the crisis, the U.S. dollar had begun to depreciate, helping to invigorate the U.S. export sector and reduce the current account deficit. Cline (2009) finds that U.S. net exports increase by 1 per cent of GDP for each 7 per cent depreciation of the dollar (real, trade-weighted). Thus, rebalancing of 2007 demand (that is, increasing net exports by 2.2 per cent of GDP) would require an approximately 15 per cent depreciation of the dollar from 2007, when the U.S. dollar was around 1.40 euro. After briefly appreciating during the crisis, the U.S. dollar returned to approximately 1.50 euro at the end of 2009, or about half-way to what Cline projects would be sufficient for the necessary expenditure shifts.

BOX 1.1
Rebalancing China's Economy*

After three decades of remarkable reforms, more than 95 per cent of China's goods and services transactions are now conducted in free markets. But factor markets remain distorted and create a "China Puzzle": disproportionate success in the outward-oriented sectors of the economy and investment, but more sluggish growth of household incomes and consumption. Factor market liberalization is now needed to complete the reforms and to drive the next wave of Chinese development.

Labour markets are still highly segmented because of the household registration system (HRS), which was originally introduced to restrict labour mobility. Today it no longer prevents farmers from moving to cities, but remains an important form of discrimination against them. Migrant workers receive only half or less compensation than their urban cousins receive for similar jobs. Capital markets are also tightly managed. Capital account restrictions are more stringent for outflows than for inflows, and for long-term than for short-term investment. Interest rates remain regulated by the central bank and the currency appears undervalued. One indicator of these distortions is the large gap between long-term government bond yields (3–4 per cent in 2009) and the nominal growth potential (around 12 per cent).

Land is owned by collectives in the countryside and by the state in cities. With the exception of property development, investors often get land at low rents or even for free in order to attract investment. The government also controls energy prices: when crude oil prices peaked at US$150 per barrel in 2008, domestic prices only rose to US$80. Lax implementation of environmental regulations leads to widespread environmental damage.

These distortions generally lower input costs, increase profits and investment returns, and improve the competitiveness of Chinese exports. They are equivalent to a producer subsidy, which we estimated at 7.2 per cent of GDP in 2008. They boost GDP but restrain the growth of wages and household income.

---

*Contributed by Professor Yiping Huang of Peking University and the Australian National University. Additional detail is provided in Yiping Huang, "China's Great Ascendancy and Structural Risks: Consequences of Asymmetric Market Liberalization", Working Paper No. 2009003, China Center for Economic Research, Peking University, 2009.

The government began to address these issues in 2003 but has had limited success so far. Solutions such as currency appreciation and social welfare systems can be effective only as part of a broad policy strategy. The fundamental focus must be the liberalization of the factor markets, including abolishing the HRS, developing the social welfare system, establishing market-based interest rates and exchange rates, and liberalizing energy prices.

In Asia, where rebalancing will require lower net exports, resources would have to move from tradable sectors to non-tradable ones, and especially to services. Asian economies have performed less well in service production than in manufacturing. (There are important exceptions, such as business and financial services in Singapore.) Restrictions on competition — from large and/or foreign firms — are often cited as a cause. In addition to exchange rate flexibility, the following strategies can also promote the development of non-tradable supply:

- *Eliminating incentives to export.* Asian export industries have at times benefited from special access to finance, investments in trade-related infrastructure, and favourable tax treatment. Non-tradables have typically lacked such support.
- *Removing barriers to competition.* Service sectors in many Asian economies face wide-ranging regulations and restrictions on entry, especially by larger companies and foreign competitors.
- *Expanding the provision of public goods and services.* Unmet needs are growing for public goods and services in health, education, environmental conservation and infrastructure development. Substantial shares of such expenditures are non-tradable.

A history of remarkable growth in tradables — and a body of academic literature — suggest that giving preference to tradable sectors is advantageous in the early stages of development. Yet macroeconomic conditions today argue against over-reliance on tradable sectors for growth. Levelling the playing field for non-tradable sectors, in turn, could generate productivity gains that will remain important drivers of growth as Asia's economies move to higher income levels.

BOX 1.2
Logistics Reform as an Engine of Gowth*

Logistics activities manage the flow of goods from point of origin to destination, as well as the associated information flows and storage. They add value by helping producers to meet customer requirements better and at lower cost. A competitive, efficient logistics sector can generate wide-ranging benefits as a source of productivity growth, economic integration and employment.

Logistics is a relatively new sector and its composition continues to evolve. It is not listed in the classification of services used in the WTO-GATS. Its original activities focused on transport and storage, but now logistics providers also offer varied management services. WTO members wanting to make commitments on logistics still have to check a list of activities rather than one code for the whole sector.

Logistics generates productivity growth in two stages. In the first, specialists emerge to provide logistical services in larger scale operations, allowing contracting firms to concentrate on their own area of competitiveness and thus become more productive. The services provided by logistics firms also lower wastage rates and inventory costs. In a second stage, contracting becomes more extensive, with greater coordination and sharing of data along the supply chain. The activities along the chain come to be regarded as integrated sets rather than independent sequential events. Exploiting efficiencies in reorganizing these processes can add to productivity.

Logistics services have important contributions to make in connecting the rest of the economy to world markets. Logistics providers help lower transport costs and accelerate integration. In agriculture, these benefits may transfer directly to the incomes of small producers.

The logistics sector is itself an important source of employment; a recent report suggests that logistics might account for 13 per cent of GDP in a developing economy, trailing off to 8 per cent in developed economies. As

---

*Contributed by Professor Christophe Findlay of the University of Adelaide. Further information is provided by De Souza, R.M. Goh, S. Gupta and L. Lei (2007), "An Investigation into the Measures Affecting the Integration of ASEAN's Priority Sectors: Phase 2: The Case of Logistics', REPSF Project No. 06/001d, and by Claire Hollweg, and Marn-Heong Wong, "Measuring Regulatory Restrictions in Logistics Services", ERIA Discussion Paper Series, ERIA-DP-2009-14 May.

industrialization proceeds and more transactions take place in urban markets, there are advantages to reorganizing production into supply chains. Inputs employed in logistics then tend to grow faster than GDP. But as productivity grows in the logistics sector and complementary inputs such as IT services and telecommunications become more extensive, input growth in logistics may slow and its share of GDP fall.

The shape of this "upside down U" is likely to be flatter the greater the reform of domestic regulation in infrastructure sectors and the greater the openness of the logistics sector itself. There is evidence that in many economies logistical services remain significantly restricted and that these restrictions adversely affect the performance of the logistics sector as measured by the World Bank Index. Not only infrastructure policy matters but also government processes such as customs. The significance of logistics is increasingly appreciated in developing countries, where for example ASEAN has identified that sector as an integration priority.

Growth Engines to Drive Recovery

Some sectors and growth processes invariably stand out as "growth engines"[6] in times of rapid expansion. These reflect unusual productivity or demand changes and create new opportunities for investment and employment. Until 2008, U.S. consumption demand was arguably *the* engine of world growth, supported by others that included foreign direct investment in China, Vietnam and other economies; real estate booms in Singapore, Indonesia and Thailand; and agricultural and mining investments in Australia and New Zealand. In addition to direct economic effects, growth engines contribute to investor psychology by making economic development comprehensible and palpable.

A growth engine is any *significant profit opportunity that leads to robust investment and economic activity*. A growth engine may generate further profit opportunities in the process of its operations, but at a minimum it is sufficiently large and long-lived to affect macroeconomic results. In this discussion, we focus on a substantial number of activities that could generate global investments of US$100 billion or more in five years. Growth engines may be launched by technological breakthroughs, such as the diffusion of the Internet in the 1990s, or by new trends, such as the ageing of populations in Asia. Some are created by policy changes.

BOX 1.3
Promoting Labour Mobility*

Several high income economies in the Asia-Pacific are experiencing low or even negative population growth because of an extended period of low fertility. Thus, an increasingly small working age population needs to support an increasingly large non-working age population ("population ageing"). In contrast, low income economies have experienced fertility declines more recently and are still enjoying a "demographic dividend" as high fertility cohorts enter the workforce while the number of dependent children and aged persons remains small. Labour mobility between these groups of countries could raise productivity and growth in the region as a whole.

Considerable cross-border migration is already taking place. Some economies have seen significant emigration (e.g., Mexico and the Philippines) while others have received significant numbers of immigrants (e.g., Australia, Canada and the United States). Some record emigration and immigration (e.g., Malaysia and Thailand). But others (e.g., Korea and Japan) remain less open to accepting significant numbers of foreign workers.

There are benefits and costs to cross-border migration. Economic theory suggests that labour mobility improves the allocation of resources (though free trade in goods and services to some extent substitutes). This does not mean that each country benefits equally. Labour migration could dampen the demographic dividend of an emigration country, especially when the emigrants are highly skilled ("brain drain"). At the same time, emigrant workers will send remittances home and may encourage foreign investment from host countries. And when they return, they will bring back technical skills, entrepreneurships, and the working culture of an industrial society.

Japan and other East Asian countries will experience rapid ageing of their populations over the coming years and would benefit from receiving a substantial number of foreign workers, both as immigrants and as temporary workers. Declining populations mean a shrinking domestic market, which

---

*Contributed by Professor Shinji Takagi of Osaka University. Further information may be found in Asian Development Bank, 2009, "Maximizing the Benefits of Labor Flows", *Asian Development Outlook 2009 Update: Broadening Openness for a Resilient Asia* (2009), pp. 67–72, and Graeme Hugo and Soogil Young, eds., *Labour Mobility in the Asia-Pacific Region: Dynamics, Issues and a New APEC Agenda*. Singapore: Institute of Southeast Asian Studies and PECC, 2008.

discourages domestic investment. Labour constraints may also directly limit the expansion of production at home. All this would leave the stock of productive infrastructure in high income countries underutilized. To be sure, there are costs that the host society must pay to accommodate foreign workers and their families who may bring a different cultural heritage.

There is increasing awareness of both opportunities and challenges from greater labour migration. Regional cooperation is important for ensuring that foreign workers' rights are protected, that migration channels are kept open when recession hits the host countries, and that pension benefits and health protection are provided to foreign workers. If well managed, international labour mobility can serve as an engine of growth and help spread prosperity across the region.

Rebalancing global demand and supply will itself create new engines of growth. Demand and price incentives for net exports in the deficit economies, including depreciated real exchange rates, will expand export- and import-competing industries. For example, U.S. exports could increase rapidly — as in the years prior to the crisis when the dollar was depreciating — in industries such as medical technology, high-technology manufacturing, and services from communications and entertainment to finance. Demand from rapidly growing Asia could drive growth in agriculture and primary goods production in Southeast Asia, Australia, New Zealand and even South America and the United States. New opportunities will emerge to establish centres to serve Asia's rapidly growing markets for financial, education, health and entertainment services.

In addition, a wide range of possible engines could directly promote balanced growth. The triggers might include freeing up competition and investment, as in Asia's logistics and other service industries. It could be also launched by new regulations in environmental protection, energy conservation and safety. Governments might also solve various "coordination problems" to generate growth, for example, by concluding major trade agreements, or setting standards that integrate domestic markets. Governments can also directly stimulate production by mandating, funding or subsidizing activities such as education and health services.

Despite the great diversity of the Asia-Pacific, recent years have seen convergence on economic and social priorities. Virtually all economies have policy initiatives in four areas:

- Economic integration: investments in connectivity and trade agreements that strengthen Asia-Pacific markets.
- Green economy: investments in energy conservation, research and development, efficient irrigation, and energy-saving vehicles and transport systems.
- Social priorities: investments in education, health care, pensions and social safety nets.
- Knowledge and productivity: investments in research and development and technology, and reforms to drive productivity.

Regional and domestic initiatives on these priorities could reinforce each other and generate new poles of growth. They would also support

---

BOX 1.4
Green Growth: South Korea's Strategy*

At the sixtieth anniversary of the founding of the Republic of Korea on 15 August 2008, President Lee Myung-bak proclaimed "low carbon green growth" as the country's new long-term vision for economic growth. Using less and cleaner energy, green growth aims to pursue three objectives simultaneously: (1) to create a synergistic relationship between environmental protection and economic growth, (2) to enhance the quality of life for the people, and (3) to contribute to global efforts to fight climate change. The National Assembly is expected to enact shortly a Framework Law on Green Growth to provide the legal and institutional basis for aligning all national and local rules with this overarching vision. The legislation will provide for an emission trading system and carbon taxes, among other things.

The government's "National Strategy for Green Growth" covers the period 2009–50 and articulates ten objectives:

(1) Mitigate greenhouse gas emissions;
(2) Enhance energy independence by reducing dependence on fossil fuels;

---

*Contributed by Dr Soogil Young, Korea's Presidential Commission on Green Growth and Chairman of the Korea National Committee for Pacific Economic Cooperation (KOPEC).

(3) Strengthen the capacity to adapt to climate change;
(4) Develop green technologies to create new growth engines;
(5) "Green" the existing industries and promote green industries;
(6) Upgrade the industrial structure for higher value-added;
(7) Create the infrastructures for a green economy;
(8) "Green" the land and the transportation system;
(9) Bring a green revolution into daily living; and,
(10) Become a role model internationally as a leader of green growth.

Under these objectives, the National Strategy proposes fifty specific action agendas. For example, under objective (4) Korea intends to promote new energy sources such as fuel cell, clean coal, and hydrogen, as well as renewable sources such as solar (photovoltaic and thermal), bio, wind, hydraulic, ocean, wastes, and geothermal.

To ensure implementation, the government has revived the developmental-era tradition of planning and formulated a Five-Year Plan for Green Growth for 2009-13. Under this plan, the government will spend about 2 per cent of annual GDP, double the amount recommended by the UN Environmental Program, on the construction of green physical infrastructures and on research and development of new and renewable energy technologies. Initially, large infrastructure investments are planned, including a project to restore four major rivers. As the economy recovers, however, the R&D portion will be increased. According to projections, the green growth plan will add 1.5–1.8 per cent to Korea's 2009 GDP and will generate employment equivalent to 26.0–32.4 per cent of the total unemployed labor force in the first quarter of 2009.

To drive this vision, President Lee announced an emissions reduction target of 30 per cent relative to 2020 emissions, the maximum recommended by the UNFCCC for the developing countries. It intends to pursue this voluntary and unilateral target independently of the outcome of the Copenhagen conference. Korea has also launched efforts to contribute to green growth in developing countries. Its ODA will increase from 0.09 per cent of income in 2008 to 0.25 per cent in 2015, with the green growth component rising from 14 per cent to more than 20 per cent. Further, Korea has launched an East Asian Climate Partnership Program with a commitment of US$200 million and intends to provide leadership for green growth for the developing countries by establishing a Global Green Institute, and an Asian Forestry Cooperation Organization in Korea. Korea will also be a lead participant in the OECD's three-year project on green growth which was launched in 2009 at Korea's proposal.

rebalancing by stimulating Asian demand, opening new markets for Asian manufactures, and cushioning the impact of declining consumption in the United States. Table 1.2 identifies sectors targeted in the regional policy discussions. Many of these initiatives have already been extensively researched and action plans are available; in some cases, there also exist good models to be emulated. In other words, blueprints often exist, providing a basis for early action.

Creating new engines of growth was, at best, a side-effect of stimulus packages introduced during the crisis. Stimulus spending did sometimes target relevant initiatives, but was not designed to address long-term, structural objectives. Indeed, governments typically sought to make policies timely, targeted (on direct spending), and temporary (the "three Ts" enunciated in the United States). This approach maximized impact, but sacrificed long-term productivity.

In contrast, forward-looking, structural initiatives need to be prioritized, productive, and persistent ("three Ps"). This report cannot do justice to their promise or complexity, but argues that they should rise on the international cooperation agenda. International policy discussions can help to forge consensus — among governments, investors, and the public — about economic priorities and directions. Common goals could stimulate innovation and investment, and strengthen domestic commitments to coherent reforms.

International Cooperation

The crisis has intensified the need for international cooperation, including managing the exit from stimulus policies and deploying structural policies. It has also established emerging economies as full partners in these decisions, due to their weight in the global economy and especially the post-crisis recovery. Credible international mechanisms for cooperation are necessary to reduce uncertainty about policy, which in turn is a prerequisite for vigorous private investments.

Several areas of cooperation are urgent and some appear to require new or substantially restructured institutions. The system of global cooperation is in flux, and will most likely evolve into a "layered" structure, with higher-level global institutions setting broad strategy and regional or bilateral institutions handling the implementation of concrete initiatives. In the following, we sketch priorities for the Asia-Pacific.

TABLE 1.2
Priorities and Growth Engines

Priorities	Growth Engines	Project Examples
Economic integration	• New frameworks for trade and investment • Investments in transport and communications infrastructure	• Doha Development Agenda • Chiang Mai Initiative Multilateralized • Regional FTAs • Pan-Asian railway network • Immigration
Green economy	• Clean energy • Energy conservation • Safe air and water	• Intelligent power grid • Electric car • Efficient irrigation • Energy efficiency (achieving Japanese standards)
Social priorities	• Affordable health care • Improved access to education • Income security • Services for the aged	• Rural health care • Free education • U.S. health reform • Pension reform
Know-how and productivity	• Financial sector development • Service sector reform • Investments in science and technology	• Information systems for health care • New green revolution

Macroeconomic cooperation. Domestic policies affect global balances and risks and call for surveillance and consultation. Shared analysis enables policy-makers to set consistent targets for fiscal and monetary policies and to minimize the volatility of variables (such as long-term real interest rates and real exchange rates) that affect investment and production. A rigorous framework for analysis and discussion of conditions in all economies, including the largest, has to be the basis for this process. Capital flows represent an especially difficult challenge. While the rebalancing issues discussed in this report are especially urgent, excessive surges of capital flows present other problems and need continuing attention. The G-20 has tasked the IMF, which already conducts regular consultations with member economies, with providing analytical support for macroeconomic assessments. Similar processes might be of value also in Asian frameworks, including the Chiang Mai Initiative Multilateralized (CMIM).

Financial risk. Coherent regulation of global financial markets would reduce a major source of market uncertainty, but will be difficult to achieve. Macro-prudential risk — the tendency for risk appetites to rise at the peak of the business cycle and to decline at the trough — has become better understood as a result of the crisis, and some governments are now likely to adopt policies (such as counter-cyclical reserve requirement adjustments) to countervail fluctuations in risk appetites. Micro-prudential risks, managed through the regulation of individual financial institutions, are also better understood. The key challenge is to improve oversight of systemically important institutions (institutions "too big to fail") and to extend regulations to all significant financial institutions and transactions. This in turn requires close cooperation among regulators from different economies in overseeing institutions that operate in multiple markets. The Financial Stability Board may help to address issues related to regulatory cooperation.

Liquidity support. Economies facing shocks have urgent financial needs. The IMF normally meets such needs in order to provide resources for adjustment, and to contain international contagion. In the wake of the 1997–98 crisis, however, borrowing from the IMF became politically unacceptable to many Asian economies. Liquidity support is central to rebalancing demand, since the perceived lack of such insurance is one reason why some Asian economies have built large foreign exchange reserves. Some new options are now emerging. In 2008–09, bilateral swaps among central banks, made available to Asian economies by the United States, China and Japan, provided emergency support for Korea, Indonesia and other economies. Recent steps to multilateralize and strengthen the Chiang Mai Initiative represent a further addition to the toolkit. Also important are global initiatives to strengthen the IMF (including through new SDR allocations), to reform its governance structure, and through these and other measures to make engagement with the IMF more acceptable politically.

Trade. Some protectionist measures have emerged in recent months, including a significant rise in administrative actions, such as the U.S. decision in September 2009 to impose safeguard tariffs on tyre imports from China. But on the whole, the measures have affected a small share of trade and have remained within the bounds of WTO disciplines. In fact, some observers have noted the absence of major protectionist surge despite the severity of the economic downturn — the "dog that didn't bark" — and argue that restraint has so far avoided the mistakes that led to disaster in the 1930s (Baldwin and Evenett 2009). Arguably, the WTO has provided a legal framework for managing the pressures that inevitably arise in serious recessions. WTO and World Bank monitoring have been instrumental in keeping protectionism at bay. But it is too soon to declare victory against protectionism, and avoiding severe disruptions in trade is in any case too modest a goal. The completion of the Doha Round and/or broad, inclusive regional FTAs could substantially improve the long-term prospects of the world economy and thus contribute immediately to the recovery.

Social priorities. Convergence of priorities on social concerns across issues such as health, environment and poverty, enables economies to pursue political goals more effectively in the framework of regional cooperation. Such cooperation could also advance economic objectives by focusing public and private investments on specific new engines of growth.

These five areas of cooperation define a complex agenda, spanning many governments and institutions. Not all issues have to be addressed at once, but early, concrete actions could help to restore confidence in Asia-Pacific integration, and thus energize private investment and entrepreneurship. Such discussions inevitably lead to a call for political will and leadership, but circumstances today make this call more urgent than ever.

V. TIME FOR DECISIONS

The crisis of 2008–09 has not become Great Depression II, but has been severe and continues to pose risks. It also represents a watershed in economic history. It offers an opportunity to address weaknesses in the global economy, to reinvent the institutions to manage interdependence, and to establish the foundations for inclusive, balanced, sustained growth. Achieving these will require:

- Adopting policies (especially in China, Japan and the United States) to keep current account imbalances across the Pacific under 3 per cent of U.S. GDP;

- Intensifying macroeconomic cooperation to chart clear policy directions and to create a predictable framework for currency and asset markets;
- Intensifying microeconomic cooperation to launch effective structural measures on financial regulation, trade liberalization, and productivity growth;
- Identifying common social priorities and fostering engines of growth to stimulate innovation, investment and employment, in the spirit of deeper regional cooperation.

The costs of failure are large. Given the damage they have already suffered, people across the region cannot afford another crisis or even a prolonged slowdown. The gains from IBS growth are equally large: the Asia-Pacific's dynamism, diversity and resources are primed to lead global growth for decades to come.

ANNEX

Definition of Sub-regions

The report covers data for the twenty-one economies that are members of the Pacific Economic Cooperation Council. To make the analysis manageable, these economies are grouped into five sub-regions as shown in the table below. The classification is based on similarities in the structural challenges that various types of economies faced during the crisis as well as geographical contiguity.

Group	Economies
China	China excluding Hong Kong SAR; Hong Kong SAR
Advanced Asia	Australia; Japan; Korea; New Zealand; Singapore; Chinese Taipei;
Southeast Asia Developing Economies	Brunei Darussalam; Indonesia; Malaysia; Philippines; Thailand; Vietnam
North America	Canada; Mexico; United States
South America	Chile; Colombia; Ecuador; Peru

Notes

1. Some of these programmes, including the mutual fund guarantee programme, were exited by the end of 2009.

2. The line blurs between rescue efforts by central banks and fiscal programmes. The IILS data do not include, for example, the US$700 billion "troubled assets relief program" (TARP), signed into law on 3 October 2008. This is a government budget item, but initially involved only loans to financial institutions that are similar to those offered by central banks in the United States and elsewhere. In late 2009, however, President Obama proposed using leftover TARP funds for wider spending purposes.

3. The plan is contained in the leaders' statement: http://www.pittsburgh summit.gov/mediacenter/129639.htm.

4. The IMF also projects a substantial increase in the world's "surplus". Although such a surplus is partly due to measurement errors, the IMF's projected increase more likely reflects inconsistencies in its several country projections.

5. Real exchange rate movements may be achieved through nominal exchange rate movements or changes in price levels. For example, a deficit economy could depreciate its currency, or keep its nominal exchange rate fixed and undergo deflation to reduce the prices of its tradable goods. If nominal exchange rates are permitted to move, they tend to adjust more rapidly, and with lower adjustment cost, than price levels.

6. A staple of growth theory, growth engines attempt to single out the main drivers of growth from the many factors at play. For example, Schumpeter (1942) saw entrepreneurial innovation as an engine; Kaldor (1957) focused on investment in industry; Hirschman (1959) and Nurske (1953) emphasized economies of scale and sectoral imbalances; and Kravis (1970) focused on trade. Contemporary endogenous growth theory (Romer 1986) emphasizes accumulated knowledge and the related processes of research and innovation.

References

Asian Development Bank. *Asian Development Outlook*. Various issues.

Bergsten, C. Fred. "The Dollar and the Deficits". *Foreign Affairs*, November/ December 2009.

Claessens, Stijn, M. Ayhan Kose and Marco E. Terrones. "What Happens During Recessions, Crunches and Busts?". International Monetary Fund, Washington, 2009.

Cline, William R. "Long-Term Fiscal Imbalances, U.S. External Liabilities, and Future Living Standards". In *The Long-Term International Economic Position of the United States*, edited by C. Fred Bergsten. Special Report 20. Washington: Peterson Institute for International Economics, 2009.

Eichengreen, Barry and Kevin H. O'Rourke. "A Tale of Two Depressions". <http://www.voxeu.org/index.php?q=node/3421>, 2009.

Elmeskov, Jorgen. "What is the economic outlook for OECD countries? An interim assessment". OECD, Paris, 2009.

Hirschman, Albert O. *The Strategy of Economic Development*. New Haven: Yale University Press, 1958.

International Monetary Fund. *World Economic Outlook*. Various issues.

Kaldor, Nicholas. "A Model of Economic Growth". *Economic Journal* 67 (December 1957): 591–624.

Kawai, Masahiro and Fan Zhai. "China-Japan-United States Integration Amid Global Rebalancing: A Computable General Equilibrium Analysis". *Journal of Asian Economics* 20, no. 6 (November 2009): 688–99.

Khatiwada, Sameer. "Stimulus Packages to Counter the Global Economic Crisis: A Review". Discussion Paper 196, International Institute of Labor Studies, 2009.

Kravis, Irving B. "Trade as a Handmaiden of Growth: Similarities between the Nineteenth and Twentieth Centuries". *The Economic Journal* 80, no. 320 (December 1970): 850–72.

Lucas, Robert. "In defence of the dismal science". *The Economist*, 6 August 2009.

Nurkse, Ragnar. *Problems of Capital Formation in Underdeveloped Countries*. New York: Oxford University Press, 1953.

Petri, Peter A. "Rebalancing Asia Pacific Expenditures: Are Major Structural Changes Required?". Paper presented at the Conference on Trade and Industry in Asia Pacific: History, Trends and Prospects, organized by The Australian National University and La Trobe University, Canberra, 19–20 November 2009.

Prasad, Eswar S. "Rebalancing Growth in Asia". NBER Working Paper 15169. National Bureau of Economic Research, Cambridge, 2009.

Romer, Paul M. "Increasing Returns and Long-run Growth". *Journal of Political Economy* 94 (1986): 1002–37.

Schumpeter, Joseph A. *Capitalism, Socialism and Democracy*. New York: Harper and Row, 1942.

Woetzel, Jonathan, Janamitra Devan, Richard Dobbs, Adam Eichner, Stefano Negri and Micah Rowland. *If You've Got It, Spend It: Unleashing the Chinese Consumer*. Seoul: McKinsey Global Institute, 2009.

2

China: Achieving Sustained Growth

Yiping Huang

I. HOW THE CRISIS AFFECTED CHINA

Aggressive fiscal and monetary policies helped to reverse the slide of the Chinese economy quickly, and growth rate in 2009 eventually exceeded the government's original target of 8 per cent. The year-on-year growth rate of GDP rose to 7.9 per cent in the second quarter of 2009 from 6.1 per cent in the first quarter, while annualized quarter-on-quarter growth confirmed an even earlier rebound, from 0.4 per cent in the fourth quarter of 2008 to 6.2 per cent in the first quarter of 2009 and 14 per cent in the second quarter (see Figure 2.1).

The speedy pick-up of the Chinese economy took many investors by surprise. In retrospect, such "surprise" was caused by two main factors. First, towards the end of 2008, manufacturers quickly reduced levels of inventories due to collapsing commodity prices and growing uncertainty of global economic outlook. This de-stocking implied that production decelerated even faster than the underlying demand. Second, there was scepticism about Chinese government's ability to turn around the economy. The common reasoning was that, after thirty years of economic reform,

FIGURE 2.1
China's Real GDP Growth
(% yoy and % qoq, saar)

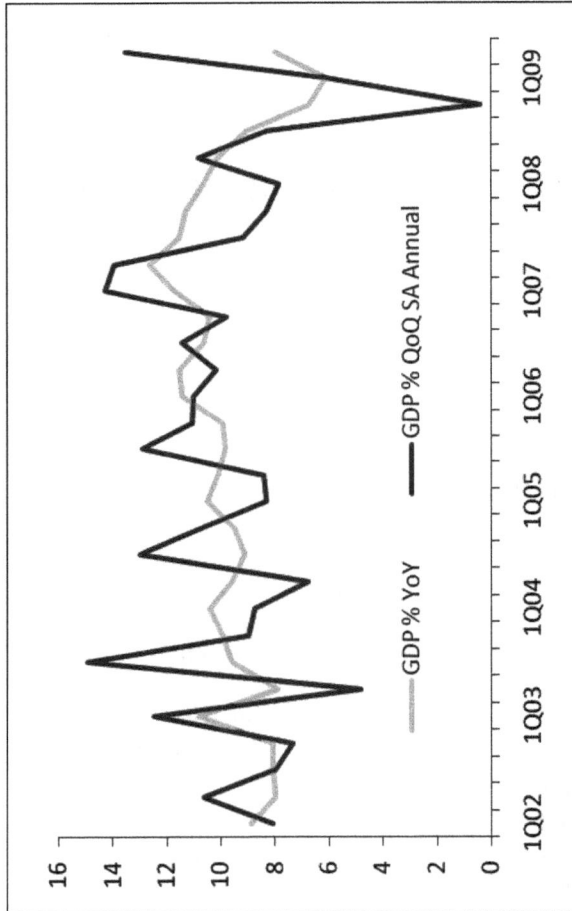

Source: CEIC Data Company and author's estimates.

the Chinese economy had become a lot more market-oriented. Therefore, the government's ability in influencing economic activities probably diminished over time.

In retrospect, such pessimism about the near-term outlook for the Chinese economy was overdone. Clearly, the de-stocking process cannot continue forever. Once manufacturers start to rebuild inventories, production could accelerate rapidly. More importantly, while the Chinese economy has become more market-oriented, the government's ability in mobilizing resources actually strengthened, not weakened, during the past years. This is evidenced by rising share of government revenue of GDP, improving quality of bank assets, improving current account position, growing foreign exchange reserves and improving profitability of the state-owned enterprises, at least during the past decade.

During the past quarters, unusual fiscal and monetary policies worked together to reverse the declining trend of the economy. The RMB4 trillion announced by the State Council in November 2008 provided a cornerstone for the government's stimulus policy. The combined investment plans proposed by provincial governments was even bigger, at RMB18 trillion according to one account. These are probably the largest stimulus policies in human history. Monetary policy expansion was equally astonishing. During the first half of 2009, commercial banks' new loans amounted to RMB7.4 trillion, almost 150 per cent of the central bank's target for the entire 2009.

China was the first to come out of growth recession among the world's major economies. And the unusual policy actions mean that Chinese growth probably will stay on strong path in the coming year or two. There is little risk that the Chinese government will not achieve its growth target of 8 per cent. The fast rebound of Chinese growth was positive news not only for China but also for the whole world. It injected much-needed support to confidence worldwide. The international commodity markets, for instance, began to stabilize and even improve, after months of weakening.

China will most likely be able to sustain strong growth over the period 2009–14, although it has to deal with some tough short-term and long-term challenges. The IMF has been consistently too pessimistic about Chinese growth for 2009–10 during the current crisis, but its forecast of growth returning to 10 per cent level after 2010 seems plausible.

II. ECONOMIC DIFFICULTIES ARE NOT YET OVER

It is important to recognize that while China's GDP growth picked up quickly, economic difficulties are not yet over. First, the export outlook probably will not improve any time soon. During the first half of 2009, exports declined at a 20 per cent pace. Recovery of export growth will probably be a slow process, as recovery of major industrial economies is likely to be slow-paced. Although the U.S. economy has also turned around, its future expansion will probably involve improvements in net exports, i.e., less imports but more exports. More importantly, American households are likely to increase their saving rates after the financial crisis, which means in the future China's export markets may not be as strong as they were a few years ago.

Second, the slow recovery of exports implies a persistence of the overcapacity problem. Since exports are already 35 per cent of GDP, their continued decline at above 20 per cent paces inevitably generates significant overcapacity problems in the Chinese economy. This is most clearly evident in the Pearl River Delta and Yangtze River Delta, China's two traditional export engines. According to the People's Bank of China (PBOC), nineteen out of twenty-four Chinese industries suffered from overcapacity problems during the first quarter of 2009.

Third, while many begin to worry about inflation risks, given abundant liquidities, deflation pressures are likely to continue to dominate, at least in the perceivable future. During the past ten years, China suffered from deflation problems twice, the first time during East Asian crisis in 1998–99 and the second time during the U.S. mild recession in 2001–02. In both times, deflation was caused by export difficulties and overcapacity. If the same causation still exists, then deflation pressures are likely to be stronger and last longer this time.

Fourth, despite initial signs of momentum in the job market, an overall improvement of employment condition is likely to lag recovery of not only the Chinese economy but also the world economy. While infrastructure spending is successful in lifting GDP growth, it is probably insufficient to create enough jobs offsetting job losses in the labour-intensive export sector. Employers will probably not start to hire aggressively again before exports, consumption or private investment pick up. But these will take some time.

Fifth, in the absence of speedy improvement of the labour market, income growth could continue to slow in the coming year. In recent months, some southern provinces revised down their benchmark wage rates. While these benchmark rates are not compulsory for employers to adopt, their downward revision reflected weakening of the job markets.

Finally, overcapacity and deflation point to a dim outlook for corporate profits. Industrial profits have been declining since the beginning of 2009. They started to show improvement due to turnaround of commodity prices, but profitability of the overall manufacturing sector will probably stay weak if the export sector does not recover strongly.

III. WORSENING STRUCTURAL IMBALANCES

There is also growing worry about quality and sustainability of China's rapid growth. Since 2001, China's GDP growth has accelerated. In the meantime, structural imbalances have also deepened. In particular, policy-makers have been worried about the economy's rising dependence on exports and investment. For instance, gross investment share of GDP rose from 33 per cent in the mid-1990s to 44 per cent in 2006–07, while export share of GDP increased from 21 per cent to 36 per cent during the same period. In the meantime, the share of consumption, especially household consumption in GDP declined steadily. In recent years, investment and net exports contributed dominant shares to GDP growth.

The unusually high investment share was comparable only to those that existed briefly in Malaysia and Thailand right before the Asian financial crisis. This caused concerns about sustainability of Chinese growth, given inefficiency and overcapacity problems in the Chinese economy. In fact, during the past ten years, the government worried about overcapacity problem almost every year — from electronics to steel and from textile to automobile. In recent years, investment also became more concentrated in heavy industries which rely disproportionately on capital, energy and other commodities. They not only contributed to resource shortages worldwide but also generated limited job opportunities.

The growing export share is equally worrisome. Looking at the surface, China is merely repeating the experiences of the export-led growth model of other East Asian economies. The only difference is that China is a large country. China already accounts for 8 per cent of global exports. Recent pace of export expansion, at around 20 per cent a year, imposed significant burdens of structural adjustments on other countries. This was the primary cause of international political pressures on China, especially its exchange rate policy.

Unfortunately, the recent stimulus policies are likely to make the structural imbalance problems even worse. Investment share of GDP will probably be much higher at the end of the two-year stimulus spending period. The fact that all these investment projects were planned and implemented in such a short period also points to potential inefficiency and waste. In fact, both policy-makers and economists already started to worry about possible rise of non-performing loans in the banking sector after two years. The government's official line remains that the amount of non-performing loans would likely increase in the coming years but the non-performing loan ratio does not need to rise.

In the meantime, the recent injection of massive liquidity, evidenced by the unusual loan growth (see Figure 2.2), also started new rounds of asset price growth. The Shanghai A-share index rose from 2008's bottom of 1,664 to above 3,300 in mid-2009. Housing prices also showed consistent month-on-month growth in 2009. These upturns were likely triggered by the improving economic outlook and rising commodity prices. Liquidity was the most important driver. The asset prices have already run way ahead of the economic fundamentals and could potentially lead to another painful adjustment if bubbles continue to grow too rapidly.

IV. RISKS OF STIMULUS POLICIES

The Chinese government should be congratulated for its decisiveness in turning around the economy. But now there is also increasing risk of over-stimulating of the economy. Of course, this is not a criticism of the government policy. Only one quarter or so ago, the world was still worrying about the worst recession since the Great Depression during the twentieth century. Governments around the world were taking whatever measures possible to prevent worst case scenarios from materializing.

Now the economy has already begun to turn around. Sustainability of recovery should become a new priority of economic policy. One key side effect of the stimulus policy is investment activities dominated by the state. During the second quarter of 2009, investment contributed more than 85 per cent of GDP growth.

Large-scale investment planned and implemented by state agencies often causes concerns about investment efficiency and investment return.

FIGURE 2.2
China's Aggressive Expansion of Bank Credit
(RMB billion)

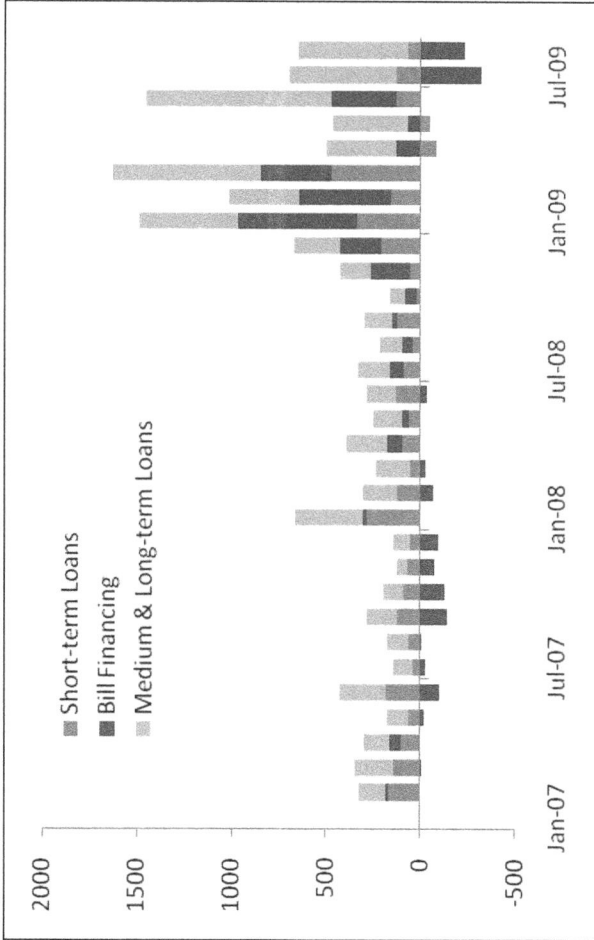

Source: People's Bank of China.

Massive state-dominated investment might lead to higher non-performing loan ratios in the banking sector in the future. More importantly, too much state investment could actually damage sustainability of growth. After all, when the stimulus policy comes to an end, exports, consumption or private investment will have to carry on growth. But very strong state investment crowds out private investment.

Another risk is that massive state investment could make it impossible for policy-makers to implement timely exit of the fiscal or monetary policies when global economic environment improves. Many of the state investment projects last for a couple of years and they cannot be terminated in the middle of construction. Therefore, if exports or consumption recover quickly, the Chinese economy could experience the overheating problem again very soon.

Monetary policy expansion is an important part of the Chinese government's responses to the crisis. Unusual credit expansion was useful in boosting investment activities. But it also started to fuel asset price bubbles, especially in the equity and housing markets. If these bubbles are left alone to grow, due to the authorities' concerns about GDP growth, China could run the risk of repeating the asset boom-and-bust experiences of the United States before the sub-prime crisis.

V. HOW TO ACHIEVE SUSTAINABLE GROWTH

Since 2003, the Chinese government has been worrying about the sustainability of rapid growth. Senior government officials have repeatedly pointed out that the current growth pattern is "unbalanced, inefficient and sustainable". The main concerns are oversized investment as a share of GDP, very large external account imbalances and inefficient resource use. The government undertook measures to improve the quality of growth, including containing investment growth, reducing incentives for exports, increasing supports to farmers and developing the social welfare system. These steps achieved some results, as evidenced by resilient consumer spending during the current global crisis.

But the task of achieving sustainable growth has not yet been accomplished. In a way, the stimulus policies made growth quality even worse. Ironically, the reason why sustainability of China's rapid growth could be at risk is precisely because the government emphasizes too much on growth itself.

In the short term, the stimulus policies may need to be fine-tuned in order to reduce policy-induced risks to growth. It is too early to end the expansionary policies now given uncertainties surrounding outlooks for both the Chinese and global economies. But if the unusual expansionary measures are left unadjusted, they could also lead to potential disruptions to the growth trajectory, via mechanisms such as crowding out of private investment or collapse of asset bubbles.

Over time, new initiatives are needed in order to achieve more sustainable growth. Clearly, international political economy dictates that the continued rise in China's export share of GDP is no longer possible. This means that domestic demand should play a greater role in driving the Chinese government going forward. It may be debatable if China can accommodate higher investment shares of GDP if quality of investment can be improved. But the declining trend of consumption share of GDP definitely needs to be reversed in the coming years.

Transition of the Chinese growth model requires a comprehensive set of new economic policies. There are three elements crucial for a successful transition: shifting the near-term policy attention from growth target to social security; moving the growth engine from manufacturing to services; and pushing forward liberalization from goods market to factor market.

Since the Asian financial crisis, 8 per cent has become a magic number for China's GDP growth. During the current financial crisis, the government again reiterated the need to maintain at least 8 per cent growth. The reason why 8 per cent growth is a must, according to government officials, is because China needs a large number of new jobs every year. Enough new jobs are a critical condition for social stability. Therefore, the ultimate rationale of the 8 per cent growth is to maintain social stability.

However, it may be a costly and risky way of achieving social stability. There should be a more effective and efficient way of doing it: providing individuals with freedom from economic fears by developing a complete social welfare system. If the government allocated higher portion of the RMB4 trillion spending package to support economic security, then perhaps GDP growth rate would become less critical. It would reduce concerns about future inefficiency and overcapacity problems. Better economic securities for households may also boost consumer spending over time.

During the past years, China earned the title of "global manufacturing centre". Manufacturing has been a key driver of Chinese economic growth. But this also has its own problems. While China still needs to create more jobs for agricultural surplus labour, rapid growth of the manufacturing sector already generated important problems such as trade frictions and environmental damages. Manufacturing activities' job elasticity may also start to decline rapidly as manufacturing moves into more sophisticated segments.

While China's manufacturing industry still has huge potential to grow, its share of GDP will probably not rise much further. The service sector should play a greater role in providing new jobs and driving economic growth. This may also require a shift of policy attention from large state-owned companies to small and medium private enterprises.

Finally, many of China's structural problems today could be attributed to distortions of the factor markets. During the reform period, policy-makers adopted an asymmetric liberalization approach: while the goods markets have almost been completely liberalized, the factor markets have remained heavily distorted. These policy distortions generally depressed costs of labour, capital, land, energy and the environment. They, like producer subsidy equivalent, increase profitability of production, raise returns to investment and improve international competitiveness of Chinese products. Meanwhile, compensation to employees as a share of GDP dropped from 52 per cent in 1997 to around 40 per cent in recent years (see Figure 2.3).

Asymmetric liberalization of markets was a key reason why, on the one hand, GDP growth was so strong, and, on the other hand, structural problems were so serious. Therefore, factor market liberalization could be a key step towards a more sustainable growth model in China.

VI. CONCLUSIONS AND RECOMMENDATIONS

The Chinese economy was hit badly by the global financial crisis, contrary to the previous popular expectation of decoupling from the United States, exports were the first victim, which account for more than 35 per cent of GDP, and are still declining at 20 per cent pace. Despite capital account controls, "hot money" inflows reversed quickly from the fourth quarter of 2008. Economic confidence was also significantly dampened, asserting further downward pressures on asset markets.

But the government successfully pulled the economy up sharply during the first half of 2009, with a massive stimulus package and aggressive credit expansion. Real GDP growth returned to close to the 8 per cent level

FIGURE 2.3
GDP Shares of Compensation, Consumption and Profits (%)

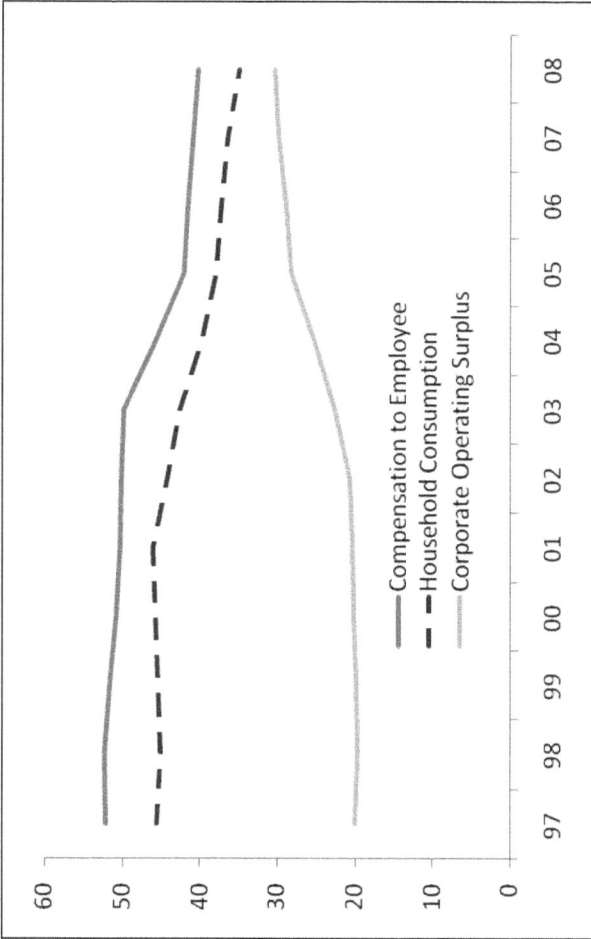

Source: National Bureau of Statistics and author's own estimation.

during the second quarter of 2009 and will likely stay above 8 per cent in the coming quarters. But the most difficult time may not yet be over as deflation could continue, unemployment rate could rise, income growth could slow, and profits could fall further.

Recently, prices of food and energy started to climb again, triggering new waves of inflation worry. However, the challenges at the micro level, particularly the persistent overcapacity problem before exports improve more dramatically, imply that inflation is not likely to become a major macroeconomic risk any time soon.

More worrying are worsening structural imbalances, as the result of the successful stimulus policy. If sustainability of rapid growth was at risk during the years preceding the current crisis, the problem became worse after the crisis. Despite strong growth during the global recession, China now faces an even tougher challenge to sustain its rapid growth in the long run. While China still needs to keep a close eye on weakness of the global economy and its likely effects on the Chinese economy, it should probably take urgent actions to improve the outlook for sustainable growth.

First, the authorities should probably adjust the credit policy to slow down the pace of loan growth. Obviously, the stimulus policy has been successful. But its reliance on bank credit in supporting growth brings its own risks, such as potential asset bubbles and non-performing loans. The new loans extended during the first half of 2009, RMB7.4 trillion, were already 150 per cent of new loans in the entire 2008. This is not likely to cause goods and service inflation any time soon. But asset bubbles are already racing ahead, particularly in the equity and housing markets. One critical question is whether the central bank should take policy action on asset prices. The conventional wisdom is negative. But if asset bubbles are primarily driven by liquidity conditions, then the central bank has to make a response, unless it is prepared to accept huge bubbles and their likely devastating consequences.

Second, policy-makers may also want to revisit composition of its stimulus spending. Infrastructure investment is the most effective way of lifting levels of economic activities. The very large number of starting projects implies that the government may not be able to unwind expansionary policies any time soon. If social stability is the main policy concern, then the authorities should perhaps make more aggressive efforts in providing the Chinese people with freedom from economic fear by increasing spending on social welfare systems. This would help not only support social stability but also balance economic structure through boosting of consumer confidence.

Third, related to this, the government may have to give up its overemphasis on GDP growth. After all, economic growth is the means of improving quality of life, not the ultimate goal of human economic activities. Many of the structural problems are rooted in the government's singled-minded pursuit of GDP growth. To change this mentality, the authorities will need to alter its over-reliance on GDP growth for assessment of government officials' performance. A few years ago, the central government started to experiment with a measure of "green GDP", which is certainly a better benchmark for assessing local officials' economic performance than the more narrowly defined GDP indicator.

Fourth, policy focus should also shift away from prioritizing large companies, especially large state-owned manufacturers, towards small and medium enterprises in the service sector. The service sector as a whole is still significantly under-represented in the Chinese economy. But it represents the future: the service sector is more resource-efficient, generates more jobs and could be the new growth engine. Government policies need to be revised to facilitate growth of small and medium enterprises in the service sector. For instance, China needs to develop a large number of small financial institutions.

Finally, liberalization of the factor markets should become the new reform priority. Distortions of factor markets and depression of factor prices are a key cause behind China's growing imbalances. The government should speed up the pace in phasing out the household registration system, which discriminates against farmers, especially migrant workers. Land should be gradually privatized where possible. Determination of energy prices are best left to the market, although the government can still use fiscal measures to support special disadvantaged groups. Urgent reforms are also needed to improve domestic capital markets, liberalize domestic interest rate and increase flexibility of exchange rate in order to improve capital efficiency.

China was the first among major global economies in ending growth recession. But the toughest test for the Chinese policy-makers may appear two years later when the stimulus spending runs out. If exports, household consumption or private investment could not step in to fill the gap of state-led infrastructure spending, then Chinese growth could fall sharply. More importantly, China's past growth model, which relies mainly on exports and investment, is not sustainable. In order to maintain rapid growth in the long run, the government must act now to improve quality of growth.

References

Huang, Yiping. "Consequences of Asymmetric Market Liberalization: China's Abnormal Ascendancy and Structural Risks". Working Paper No. 3, China Center for Economic Research, Peking University, Beijing, 2009*a*.

————. "Macroeconomic Performance amid Global Crisis". In *China's New Place in a World in Crisis*, edited by Ross Garnaut, Ligang Song and Wing Thye Woo. Canberra: ANU E-Press, and Washington, D.C.: Brookings Institution, 2009*b*.

Macroeconomic Analysis Group. "Policy Challenges after Retaining 8% Growth". China Finance 40 Forum, Beijing, 2009.

Yu Yongding. "China's Policy Responses to Global Economic Crisis and Its Perspective on the Reform of International Monetary System". Paper presented at the Asia Europe Economic Forum Conference, Kiel Institute of World Economy, Germany, 7–8 July 2009.

3

Advanced Asia:
Achieving Sustained Growth

Shinji Takagi

I. HOW THE CRISIS AFFECTED ADVANCED ASIA[1]

Although individual circumstances differed, the Advanced Asian economies of the Asia-Pacific region were all hit hard by the global financial crisis when it spread to the real sector and caused the volume of world trade to collapse in the latter part of 2008. These economies immediately responded to the sharp deceleration of economic activity by easing monetary and fiscal policies substantially, which acted relatively quickly to help stabilize the economies. In fact, signs of economic recovery were already evident in the region in the first part of 2009, with some economies returning to positive growth in the early months. The biggest policy challenge most economies faced at the end of 2009 was to decide when to reverse the extraordinary stance of monetary and fiscal policies, which cannot be sustainable for a long time, in view of potential inflationary and debt sustainability concerns.

How to manage the exit will not be easy, however, inasmuch as the prospect for the recovery of world trade remains uncertain. Over the short term, there is a danger that pulling the stimulus prematurely may cause the nascent recovery to stall. Over the medium term, there is going to be an inevitable rebalancing of global demand that will have major implications for Advanced Asia. It will take time to restore balance sheets in advanced Western countries, notably the United States, so that the region's net exports to these markets must decline. This means that Advanced Asia, especially those economies that had relied on high-tech exports to the West to propel growth, must find alternative engines of growth if it is to make the economic recovery firm and sustainable.

The initial impact of the U.S. sub-prime crisis was relatively small on the Advanced Asian economies. For the most part, these economies had only limited exposure to sub-prime-related assets and their banking systems were relatively sound and well capitalized. In fact, the biggest challenge facing these economies in the summer of 2008 was high energy and other commodity prices. This terms of trade development adversely affected Japan, Korea and Chinese Taipei, given their high dependence on energy and commodity imports. On the other hand, Australia, benefiting from the same terms of trade shock, saw strong private investment through the fall of 2008, but had to deal with an overheating economy.

Through the third quarter of 2008, the Advanced Asian economies appeared little affected by the financial crisis. Singapore registered year-on-year growth of nearly 2 per cent in the third quarter, despite the deceleration of growth in its large financial sector. Japan's economy began to contract in the second quarter, but the cause was more likely related to the fall in stock prices (which adversely affected the willingness of banks to lend), the delayed impact of the high energy and commodity prices, and the sharp appreciation of the yen against major currencies. New Zealand had already experienced a deceleration of growth as it saw an end to its real estate boom and private investment suffered. Yet, growth remained modestly positive.

It was only in the fourth quarter that output collapsed across the region (Figure 3.1). Japan, Korea and Chinese Taipei were hit hard by the global shrinkage of trade. The collapse of exports in these economies, as noted in the main report, was directly translated into a correspondingly large fall in industrial production. Korea experienced, in addition, a precipitous outflow of capital, which almost caused a currency crisis (Korea's balance of short-term external debt and foreign ownership in the equity market exceeded the size of the country's foreign exchange

FIGURE 3.1

Quarterly GDP Growth in Advanced Asian Economies (% yoy)

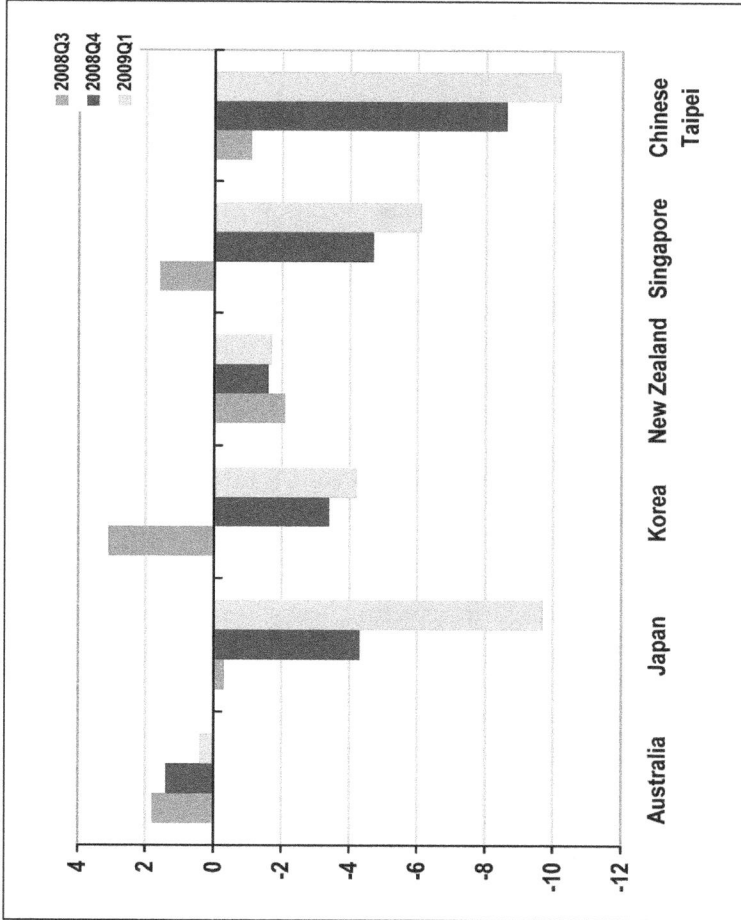

Sources: International Monetary Fund, *International Financial Statistics*, on-line database; for Chinese Taipei only, Central Bank of the Republic of China, *Financial Statistics*.

reserves, which created investor nervousness). Singapore was affected not so much by the collapse of exports as the collapse of global trade, given its large transport-related service sector, as well as the shrinkage of the financial sector.

II. WHAT CAUSED THESE EFFECTS?

The impact of the global financial crisis turned out to be greater on Japan, Korea, Singapore and Chinese Taipei than on the epicentre countries of North America and Europe, where the crisis largely started. The reasons are not difficult to find. First, these Advanced Asian economies had a structure of trade that was concentrated in highly income-elastic industrial supplies, capital goods and consumer durables. Sommer (2009) shows that economies with a greater share of advanced manufacturing in GDP tended to experience sharper output declines than others, with Singapore and Chinese Taipei at the top of the list. In addition, global trade integration increased the sensitivity of these economies to final demand developments in the rest of the world.

Second, these economies depended to a great degree on final demand in North America and Europe. While Asia's intra-regional trade had expanded significantly in the years leading to the crisis (from around 30 per cent during 1980–90 to well over 50 per cent), most of it was in trade in parts and components. Asia's intra-regional trade was the flipside of intra-regional foreign direct investment (FDI), which had created production networks in such industries as electronics, automobiles and other machinery products that cut across national borders. Under these circumstances, intra-regional trade expanded but did not lead to a decoupling of Advanced Asia from the rest of the world. Much of what was produced in the region was shipped elsewhere for final consumption.

In this context, the experience of Japan is illustrative (Kawai and Takagi 2009). Japan was affected by the shrinkage of "triangular trade" where Japan and the Asian NIEs (Korea, Singapore and Chinese Taipei) export parts and components to China and other emerging Asian economies for assembly into final products. Over 85 per cent of the decline in Japanese exports to Asia was in industrial supplies and capital goods, whereas the share for the United States and Western Europe was only 60 per cent (with the rest almost entirely accounted for by consumer durables). This means that, although Asia was Japan's biggest export market, it was not the dominant market for consumer durables. Japan's exports of industrial supplies and capital goods to emerging Asia were severely affected as demand for Japanese parts, components and capital goods — all essential inputs for the production of final consumer products — declined steeply. As a result, Japan's exports to Asia collapsed as much as its exports to the epicentre countries of North America and Europe.

Australia and New Zealand were different. They both experienced large current account deficits in recent years, which were financed by capital inflows. The global de-leveraging that followed the onset of the subprime crisis and intensified after the Lehman failure led to a drying up of liquidity, which placed contractionary pressure on their economies, while their currencies depreciated sharply. They were also affected by the adverse impact of declining commodity prices on private investment and the negative wealth effect of declining real estate prices on private consumption. To the extent that the collapse of world trade was less of a factor, their output decline was more limited and, with a recovery of commodity prices in early 2009, there were early signs of bottoming out. Australia particularly benefited from a pick-up of Chinese growth in early 2009.

III. MACROECONOMIC POLICY RESPONSES

Monetary Policy Measures

Up to the fall of 2008, most of the Advanced Asian economies were pursuing a tight monetary policy. Australia, for example, had an overheating economy, with rising commodity prices and buoyant private investment; with capital inflows, it also had a large current account deficit. The rising commodity prices meant that inflation-targeting countries, such as New Zealand and Korea, had to strike a delicate balance between curtailing inflationary pressure and addressing a possible weakening of economic activity. Singapore continued to allow its currency to appreciate in nominal effective terms.

When the real impact of the global crisis was felt, all central banks shifted to monetary easing. The subsequent softening of energy and commodity prices allowed the monetary authorities to cut policy interest rates aggressively, especially after the collapse of Lehman Brothers in

September. New Zealand was the first country to shift to monetary easing when it cut the policy rate (the official cash rate or OCR) in July 2008. From July to April 2009 the Reserve Bank reduced the OCR in several steps from 8.25 to 2.5 per cent.

Australia was the next to follow. From September 2008 to February 2009 the Reserve Bank lowered the policy rate (the cash rate) by 4 percentage points, from 7.25 to 3.25 per cent; it further cut the rate to 3 per cent in April. Likewise, Korea reduced its policy rate (the base rate) from 5.25 to 2 per cent from October 2008 and February 2009; Chinese Taipei reduced the policy rates from late September 2008 to February 2009 by about 2.4 per cent. In October 2008, Singapore shifted to a zero per cent appreciation of the nominal exchange rate, in the reversal of a policy of graduate appreciation it had followed since April 2004. In April 2009, the Monetary Authority of Singapore, while keeping the zero appreciation policy, recentred the policy band to the prevailing level of the nominal exchange rate (which represented an effective depreciation of the currency).

With Japan continuing to maintain easy monetary policy since the late 1990s, market interest rates in Advanced Asia reached historically low levels (Figure 3.2). In particular, interest rates in Japan, Singapore and Chinese Taipei approached zero, with little room left for further interest rate easing. Because the level of interest rates was low to begin with, the impact of recent monetary easing on the real economy was likely limited, at least through the conventional channel. On the other hand, the other economies had more space to cut interest rates. The pick-up of economic growth in 2009 in these economies may to some extent be attributable to the working of the conventional monetary policy transmission channel.

Some central banks resorted to "unconventional" monetary easing measures. The Reserve Bank of Australia, the Bank of Korea, and the Monetary Authority of Singapore entered into swap arrangements with the U.S. Federal Reserve, in order to address elevated pressure in the U.S. dollar short-term funding markets. Three central banks (Australia; Korea; Chinese Taipei) in late 2008 injected ample liquidity into the financial system, by expanding eligible collateral for central bank lending or the scope of counter-parties. In December 2008, the Bank of Korea also began to pay interest on required reserves in order to provide banks with incentives to lend. The Bank of Japan increased purchases of Japanese government bonds in January 2009 and again in March 2009; it began

FIGURE 3.2
Market Interest Rates in Advanced Asian Economies (% pa)

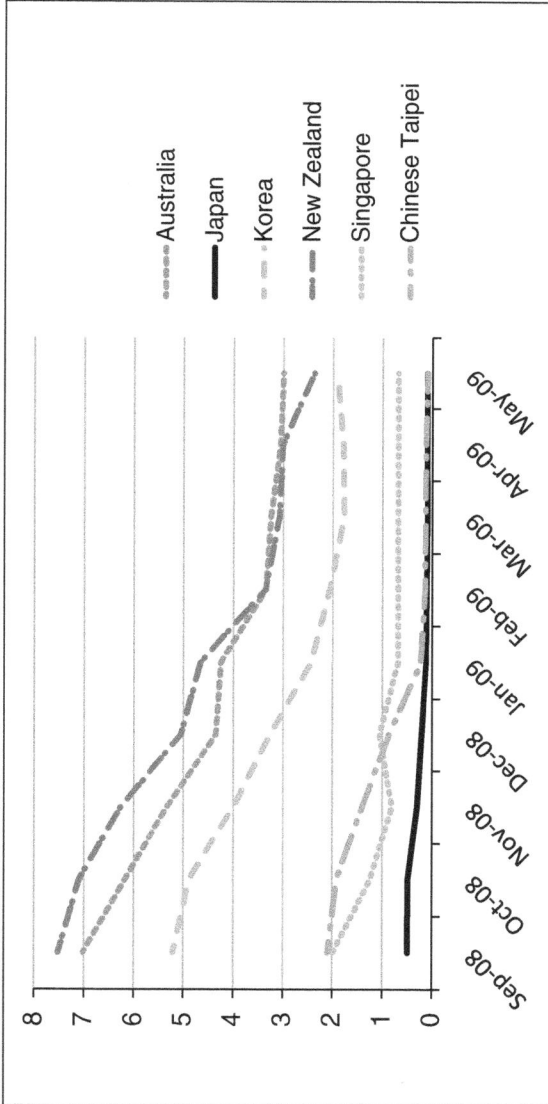

Sources: International Monetary Fund, *International Financial Statistics*, on-line database; for Chinese Taipei only, Central Bank of the Republic of China, *Financial Statistics*.

Note: For all economies, market interest rates are given by item 60b.

outright purchases of corporate bonds in February 2009 and eased collateral requirements for central bank lending on several occasions.

Fiscal Policy Measures

In late 2008, fiscal policy also turned expansionary. While in Australia and New Zealand expansionary fiscal policy was combined with easy monetary policy and currency depreciation to arrest falling output, fiscal policy needed to take a central role in other countries where the scope of further monetary easing was limited. This was especially the case with Japan, where interest rates were near zero from the outset and the currency was appreciating. The Japanese authorities eased fiscal policy substantially, despite the country's chronic large fiscal deficits and high debt-to-GDP ratio. Years of fiscal prudence allowed considerable fiscal space for Korea and Singapore.

Considerable easing of fiscal policy was evident for all economies in 2008 and 2009 and, given the announced measures, the easy stance is expected to continue in 2010. For Singapore, an over 5 per cent swing from a large surplus of previous years represents a significant reversal of policy; the fiscal position remains in surplus only because the country is drawing on the accumulated reserves from past surpluses to finance the increased fiscal spending. In late 2008, the government provided direct assistance to low-income families, special family support measures, higher payouts of Growth Dividends, and utility rebates; and introduced a programme to retain displaced workers. The FY 2009 budget further included cash grants to employers (to subsidize part of their wage bill), tax cut measures and rebates, and an accelerated capital allowance.

In other economies, too, the fiscal measures involved various types of spending increases and tax cuts. Australia and Chinese Taipei introduced tax incentives for business investment, and increased public investment in infrastructure. Japan and Chinese Taipei distributed cash transfers to stimulate personal consumption. Chinese Taipei offered a discounted sale of industrial land, increased financial support to SMEs, and subsidized households to purchase energy-saving products. New Zealand introduced personal tax cuts (staggered over three years) and increased government spending. Although New Zealand had maintained fiscal surpluses in recent years, the announced fiscal measures are expected to cause the fiscal position to turn negative in 2009 and result in a deficit of 6 per cent of GDP in 2012.

Assessing the Policy Measures

It is inherently difficult to assess the effectiveness of macroeconomic policies because, given the confluence of many external and internal factors, one cannot ascribe a change in macroeconomic performance to any one policy measure. Even so, the combination of monetary easing and fiscal expansion almost certainly supported the economies in Advanced Asia when world trade collapsed. Part of the success may well be due to their largely coordinated nature — the substantial policy easing was effected almost simultaneously not only within the region but also across the world.

In Australia, Korea and New Zealand, where the level of interest rates was sufficiently high to begin with, the monetary policy transmission channel remained unimpaired, allowing monetary easing to have its conventional impact. Combined with the impact of significant fiscal stimulus and depreciating currencies, this may explain the relatively early recovery of these economies. Korea, for example, registered a 2.6 per cent growth in the second quarter of 2009, the fastest in more than five years, while Australia grew by 1.3 per cent from the previous quarter (seasonally adjusted at an annual rate). In October 2009, Australia became the first G-20 country to raise the policy interest rate. In the other Advanced Asian economies, fiscal policy carried a greater weight. Although empirical evidence is generally sceptical of the multiplier effect of expansionary fiscal policy, direct government purchases added positively to domestic demand.

In the absence of a structural policy to create new private sector sources of demand, however, no recovery based on public-sector stimulus can be sustainable. There is thus a danger that once the stimulus is gone, so does the recovery. For one thing, fiscal space is limited in several economies. In Japan, the public debt-to-GDP ratio is so high that it is not clear to what extent fiscal expansion can be sustained. In New Zealand, the debt-to-GDP ratio is low but the country runs a perennial current account deficit, so the government may not be able to increase public debt too much further without causing interest rates to rise, as most of the debt is externally held. The available fiscal space is more limited than it appears.

Continuing the extraordinary stance of easy monetary and fiscal policies is both unrealistic and infeasible. Sooner or later, the costs of greater inflationary and debt sustainability concerns will begin to outweigh any benefits. Moreover, unconventional monetary policies and increased fiscal spending mean greater public sector intervention in the allocation of resources, which should best be left to the market during more normal times. The biggest policy challenge is to determine when and how to unwind the extraordinary stance of monetary and fiscal policies.

IV. STRUCTURAL POLICIES FOR SUSTAINING THE RECOVERY

Placing the economy on a sustainable growth path would require more fundamental action. Because it will take time to restore balance sheets in advanced economies severely affected by the financial crisis, notably the United States, the region's net exports to these markets will inevitably decline. Over the medium term, moreover, some rebalancing of global demand from deficit to surplus economies will be desirable in any case, in order to prevent the recurrence of a large global payments imbalance. Thus, from the point of view of both necessity and desirability, the economies of the region must stimulate regional and domestic demand as a substitute for demand in the advanced markets outside the region.

This does not suggest that the region's dependence on global demand in the past has necessarily been a bad thing. To the contrary, part of what happened recently is an inevitable outcome of global economic integration, which has brought enormous benefits to the region. As the global economy inevitably recovers, so will the Advanced Asian economies. However, with the United States running a smaller current account deficit, Asia must play a bigger role in the increasingly integrated world economy, by offering a bigger market for final goods produced by all regions. This is important not only to keep the region's growth momentum going, but also help the recovery of the world economy. Advanced Asia must lead the way.

Different roles are expected from different economies. For a large economy like Japan, generating its own domestic demand is critical. Japan, emerging from a decade of sub-par growth following the collapse of a domestic asset-price bubble in the late 1980s, relied on external demand to propel its growth as the yen depreciated towards a historical average level in real effective terms. The export-led growth worked well because of the expansion of the global economy. Such a strategy, however, will not work in the coming years because the United States will likely maintain smaller net imports. Japan must increasingly rely on its own domestic demand.

On the other hand, a small economy like Singapore can expect to grow only as part of a larger outside economy. Its openness, which has caused a severe collapse of output in recent months, should also allow Singapore's growth to pick up more strongly than other economies when regional and global recovery gets underway. Singapore has been addressing long-term structural issues, by building up capacity in key manufacturing and service sectors, reducing the corporate income tax rate, and making long-term investment in infrastructure, education, healthcare and R&D. These measures should help as Singapore reaps the benefits of regional and global recovery.

But all economies will benefit from a more resilient regional economy that does not rely too much on outside demand. The surest way to create more final demand within the region is to promote intra-regional trade in final goods, ideally through progress in multilateral trade liberalization at the WTO, but should that remain impossible, through the active promotion of a region-wide comprehensive free trade arrangement. Although there are a number of ASEAN-centred and bilateral free trade agreements, there is no single, comprehensive agreement that encompasses the whole region; the complex web of bilateral agreements (the so-called Asian noodle bowl) is not sufficient to create a large enough single market for final goods. It is urgent that a political decision be made to move forward the proposal — initially made by Japan in 2006 — for a Comprehensive Economic Partnership in East Asia (CEPEA), the goal of which is to create a highly integrated market encompassing not only ASEAN+3 but also India, Australia, and New Zealand, all of the countries of the East Asia Summit (EAS).

As to promoting domestic private demand, a number of alternative engines of growth are conceivable, including the promotion of investment in energy-saving technologies and renewable sources of energy (see the main report). In addition, several economies of Advanced Asia must address the problem of population ageing, which may act as a deterrent to promoting private investment targeted at the domestic market. Unless new products are introduced that invigorate demand (such as cell phones or digital television sets in the past decade), the domestic market for final goods can only be expected to shrink. Further deregulation of the service sector could remove impediments to domestic investment. To the extent socially acceptable, Advanced Asia could also consider measures to liberalize immigration in order to maintain market size (see Box 3.1). Harmonizing rules for immigration, especially on labour standards for foreign workers, should be put on the regional policy agenda in order to promote labour migration in an orderly manner. Greater labour mobility, if well managed, can benefit both the source and destination economies (see Box 1.3 in Chapter 1).

Some form of regional exchange rate cooperation should be a part of any medium-term efforts to create a larger single market. Recent empirical evidence shows that vertical integration is adversely affected by exchange rate volatility and that exchange rate stability promotes trade (Thorbecke 2008). As a highly interdependent region, moreover, the spillover effects from exchange rate volatility could be large. The need for a mechanism to minimize intra-regional exchange rate volatility became apparent during the height of the global crisis — the Japanese yen appreciated sharply against the U.S. dollar while at the same time the Korean won, the Australian dollar, the Singapore dollar, and the New Zealand dollar moved in the opposite direction (Figure 3.3). It is possible that the sharp appreciation of the Japanese yen against the region's major currencies was a factor that contributed to the severe output collapse of Japan, and placed undue burden of adjustment on the Japanese economy. The relatively early recovery of Australia, Korea and New Zealand was to some extent at the expense of Japan.

V. RECOMMENDATIONS

The extraordinary macroeconomic policy stances adopted in response to the crisis cannot be sustained for long; neither can they be expected to place economies on a sustainable growth path in the absence of more fundamental action. As the stimuli of monetary easing and fiscal expansion are inevitably withdrawn, the Advanced Asian economies must act quickly to implement structural policies to help sustain the recovery. Among the key objectives are to create a large, single market for final goods within the region and to stimulate domestic private demand.

The main report suggests a number of alternative engines of growth to achieve these objectives. This chapter has particularly highlighted the need,

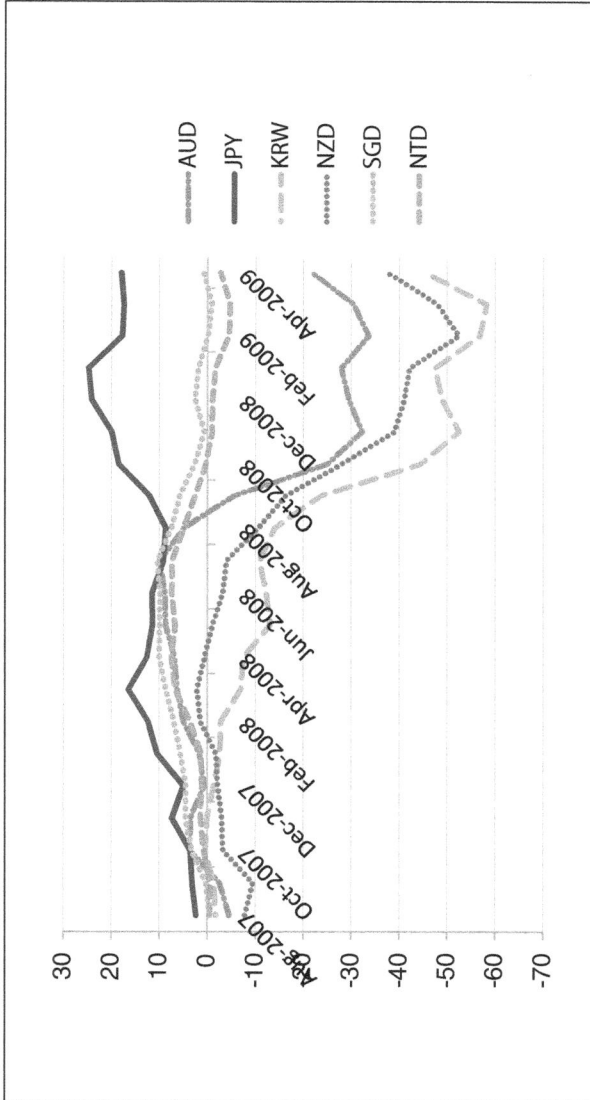

FIGURE 3.3
U.S. Dollar Exchange Rates of Advanced Asian Currencies
(% change from July 2007, monthly average rates)

Sources: International Monetary Fund, *International Financial Statistics*, on-line database; for Chinese Taipei only, Central Bank of the Republic of China, *Financial Statistics*.

BOX 3.1
Japan's Immigration Policy

Japan has long maintained a restrictive immigration policy subject to only limited efforts to liberalize immigration. In the early 1990s the Japanese government allowed the hiring of foreign workers of Japanese ancestry (mainly from South America) in order to meet the shortage of labour in manufacturing industries. Economic incentives both on the demand and supply side, however, seem to have worked to increase the number of migrant workers in recent years. United Nations data quoted by Hugo and Young (2008) show that the number of international migrants in Japan increased by about 400,000 from 2000 to 2005, an estimated half of which may well be temporary workers including students in tertiary education.

Despite the fact that the economy has been rather stagnant in recent years, labour shortage in some sectors, especially healthcare and nursing care, is acute. Responding to industry pressure, the recent free trade agreements with Indonesia and the Philippines include a provision to allow a limited number of workers to come to Japan to work in those sectors.

There is a strong social resistance to liberalizing immigration in Japan, but increasing awareness of the adverse impact of an ageing population on the economic vitality of the country is beginning to create a national debate on the issue. In 2008, the Nippon Keidanren (Japan Business Federation) and a working group of the then ruling Liberal Democratic Party proposed that up to 10 million immigrants be accepted into Japan over the coming years in order to maintain the population at current levels.

Although the newly elected government has not announced a public position towards immigration, Prime Minister Hatoyama had stated prior to assuming office in September 2009 that the subject of immigration could not be avoided in the future, implying that a political decision would need to be made to determine the manner and extent of liberalizing the entry of foreign workers into the country (*Jiji*, 11 August 2009). The government's plan, announced in 2008, to increase the number of foreign students in Japan from about 120,000 currently to 300,000 by the year 2020 can be considered a backdoor way of increasing the number of foreign workers.

---

absent progress on the Doha round of WTO negotiations, to move ahead with the proposal for a Comprehensive Economic Partnership in East Asia (CEPEA) as a way to consolidate the complex web of bilateral trade agreements. To expand the domestic market, Advanced Asia should consider measures to deregulate the service sector and to liberalize immigration. Harmonizing rules for immigration, especially on labour standards for foreign workers, should be put on the regional policy agenda in order to promote labour migration in an orderly manner. Promoting labour migration can benefit both the host and source countries.

Finally, cooperation to achieve greater intra-regional exchange rate stability would help not only to promote intra-regional trade but also to create a region more resilient to outside shocks. It will also help spread the burden of adjustment more equally across the region, as it adjusts to weaker net export demand from countries outside the region. It must be emphasized that the purpose of regional exchange rate cooperation is to increase the flexibility of the region's currencies in order to promote the needed global rebalancing, but the flexibility is with respect to the U.S. dollar and not against each other.

Note

1. Advanced Asia is defined to consist of Australia, Japan, Korea, New Zealand, Singapore and Chinese Taipei.

References

Hugo, Graeme and Soogil Young, eds. *Labour Mobility in the Asia-Pacific Region: Dynamics, Issues and a New APEC Agenda*. A Joint Study by the Pacific Economic Cooperation Council and the APEC Business Advisory Council. Singapore: Institute of Southeast Asian Studies, 2008.

Kawai, Masahiro and Shinji Takagi. "Why Was Japan Hit So Hard by the Global Financial Crisis?". Working Paper No. 153. Asian Development Bank Institute, 2009.

Sommer, Martin. "Why Has Japan Been Hit So Hard by the Global Recession?". IMF Staff Position Note 09/05. International Monetary Fund, 2009.

Thorbecke, Willem. "The Effect of Exchange Rate Volatility on Fragmentation in East Asia: Evidence from the Electronics Industry". *Journal of the Japanese and International Economies* 22 (2008): 535–44.

4

Southeast Asia:
Achieving Sustained Growth

Michael Plummer

I. HOW THE CRISIS AFFECTED SOUTHEAST ASIA

Southeast Asia was not heavily invested in high-risk "toxic" assets, but it is dependent on external demand for economic growth especially since the Asian crisis of 1997–98. The crisis also affected balance sheets and created a general liquidity shortage, especially with respect to trade finance, which abated slowly. The large drop in commodity prices during the crisis and the drop off in foreign direct investment (FDI) further contributed to Southeast Asia's downturn. Thus, while the current crisis is far less devastating than the Asian crisis of 1997–98 for most countries, it has taken a high toll.

The more externally dependent Southeast Asian economies were the hardest-hit (Figure 4.1 and, in a comparative context, Figure 1.1 of Chapter 1). The "dynamic Asian economies" of Malaysia and Thailand are both expected to contract by 3 per cent in 2009 (ADB Update 2009).[1] Indonesia, which is less open compared to the other Southeast Asian economies and whose growth in consumption compensated for the drop

FIGURE 4.1
GDP Growth (%) ASEAN Countries
(1987–2008 and Projections 2009–10)

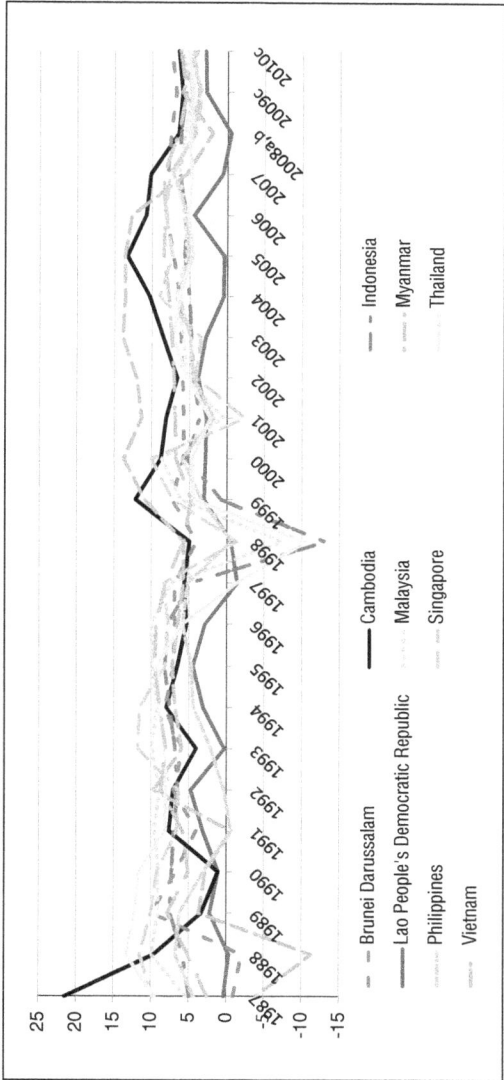

Notes: 2008 data for Brunei Darussalam and Myanmar are IMF estimates.
2009 and 2010 data are IMF forecasts.

Source: IMF, WEO, April 2009

in external demand, was able to make it through 2009 with only a slight reduction in growth. Vietnam's growth has fallen to about 3 per cent in 2009, and that of the Philippines to less than 2 per cent (ibid.). Growth trends in some of the transitional ASEAN economies are less clear; there is evidence of a significant contraction in Cambodia (–1.5 per cent projected for 2009) but in the less open economies of Lao PDR and Myanmar, growth is being sustained (e.g., at 5 per cent in Lao PDR).

The outlook for Southeast Asia depends to a large extent on the larger PECC economies avoiding an early exit from fiscal stimulus programmes. But ASEAN countries need to foster growth in internal demand as well. The stimulus packages of the ASEAN economies varied considerably and generally corresponded to the degree of economic contraction, with Malaysia, Thailand and the Philippines embarking on far more aggressive fiscal policies than Indonesia and, of course, the transitional ASEAN economies (see, for example, Figure 1.4 of Chapter 1). There has been criticism of these packages, particularly in terms of the delay in disbursement of funds. But the "time inconsistency" problem will likely not materialize; signs are that the ASEAN countries are continuing their fiscal push.

Monetary policies also tended to be expansionary in the original ASEAN countries in order to combat the crisis, but the degree of expansion was limited, given inflationary considerations and the fact that monetary independence in these developing countries is relatively limited particularly in the context of crisis. Coupled with the "flight to safety" threat that these economies face in uncertain times, overly aggressive cuts in interest rates could have led to capital flight and greater exchange rate volatility. Stricter capital controls to prevent this could have led to even greater uncertainty and potential destabilization, though this was chosen as the lesser of two evils by some countries. Thus, Southeast Asian monetary policy-makers had to follow the (U.S.) lead: After a considerable jump following the Lehman Brothers collapse, Southeast Asian interest rates were pushed down significantly through 2008, with the yield curve falling impressively for most countries, with the notable exception of Indonesia. As of end-August 2009, yields had come up significantly to what would be more "normal" levels — again with the exception of Indonesia, whose yield curve was lower end-August than it was in December 2008 — and pretty much in line with the movement of the U.S. yield curve (*Asian Bond Monitor*, September 2009).[2]

Inflation had been a problem in just about all ASEAN countries (save Brunei and Thailand) in 2008. As a region that has prided itself on conservative monetary policies, this presented a key policy challenge, especially in the first half of 2008 when the price of primary commodities increased significantly. The reduction in international and domestic demand has had the expected effect of reducing inflation and inflationary expectations considerably in the region, and estimates for 2009 are within a tolerable range for most economies. Inflation in the original ASEAN countries in 2009 is expected to be about a third of what it was in 2008, and forecast to rise only in the case of Thailand. Prospects for 2010 and 2011 are even better for all economies except Myanmar, which is expected to continue to have inflation at 20 per cent. This positive inflation news is important because it provides the region with an additional tool in its macroeconomic policy arsenal. However, keeping inflation under control in ASEAN will continue to be a priority for sustainable growth in the future.

Projections suggest that the region will return to trend growth in 2011. Hence, while Southeast Asia has managed the short-run consequences of the crisis reasonably well, it will eventually need to exit stimulus programmes and transition to long-run sustainable growth. This will require significant "rebalancing" of some of the economies, as noted in Chapter 1, and active participation in creating a more stable global financial system. The *pattern* of growth prior to the crisis was arguably unsustainable, as it was based too much on external demand, while the *rate* of growth itself was arguably sub-optimal: Growth rates prior to the Asian crisis were significantly higher than post-crisis, with investment demand growth in particular falling over the past decade (ADB 2008). We argue below that reforms designed to rebalance the Southeast Asian economies in the medium-long-term can be achieved without sacrificing growth.

II. RISKS TO SUSTAINED GROWTH AND THE NEED FOR A PROACTIVE POLICY MIX

Continuing uncertainties about the global and regional economic outlook argue for active macroeconomic and microeconomic policies. The current crisis underscored the importance of aggressive and even unorthodox macroeconomic policy measures and the need for better vehicles of economic cooperation. But post-crisis policy regimes must go beyond plugging holes that were responsible for the crisis. The policy responses of Southeast Asian countries in the aftermath of the Asian crisis are a case in point. Policy-makers were ultimately effective in reducing many shortcomings present in their financial regimes prior to the Asian crisis, but they did little to adopt necessary reforms at the microeconomic level in order to create more competitive economies (Adams 2008). The need to reduce the cost of doing business, improve the functioning of financial markets, deepen equity and fixed income markets, stimulate greater competition in the financial sector, and provide a more welcome environment for innovation constitute unfinished business. These and other policies, as outlined below, provide a forward-looking strategy that could help ASEAN emerge stronger from the current crisis. We focus on five areas: rebalancing; fiscal and monetary policy; regional economic cooperation; keeping existing and attractive new production networks; and microeconomic policy reform.

The Need to Rebalance: Strengthening Domestic Demand

While economists did not anticipate the current meltdown in its present form, they had argued that existing imbalances could not be sustained indefinitely. A U.S. current account deficit of 3 per cent could be sustainable, but the deficit was running at double that rate in recent years. How to get from 6 per cent to 3 per cent was highly controversial (see, for example, McKinsey Global Institute 2007 and Cline 2005) but the adjustment would have required a commitment on the part of both debtor and creditor countries to engineer a soft landing. The lack of such cooperation is certainly a reason for today's ongoing "hard landing".

By relying on external rather than domestic demand, Asian economies (and others) effectively made it possible for these deficit economies to finance spending binges that did, indeed, prove unsustainable. Although it would be a great exaggeration to blame Asian economies — particularly Southeast Asian economies, which after all were relatively small players — for the current crisis, this analysis does suggest that greater reliance on domestic demand, rather than net exports, would have been in their collective interest.

Southeast Asian countries could pursue a number of measures to strengthen domestic demand, some of which are discussed more at length below. First, reducing the macroeconomic bias in favour of net exports could be one vehicle, including more flexible exchange rate policies and any special microeconomic incentives that create biases in favour of exports at the expense of production for the domestic market. Second, microeconomic reform, including in the financial sector, would create a more attractive environment for investors, as well as allowing for greater "consumption smoothing" for consumers. A third and related point would be to reduce obstacles to foreign investment, particularly FDI. While freeing up short-term capital flows needs to be undertaken carefully, foreign investment can yield important benefits to the local economy, from strengthening equity and fixed income markets to facilitating technology transfer and ready access to new international markets by luring FDI. Fourth, spearheading investments in areas that are of importance to the long-term growth prospects of the country, including investment in infrastructure, education, and the like, would stimulate domestic demand as well as developing a strong foundation for future growth and development. Fifth, a greater focus on the service sector in general, which is notoriously inefficient in Southeast Asia, would have the same effect of rebalancing the economy and at the same time increasing economic efficiency.

Improving Enabling Environments for Fiscal and Monetary Policy

During the current crisis, the G-20 tried to coordinate to some degree fiscal and monetary policy responses to the crisis. The outcome was arguably disappointing: countries tended to go their own way in terms of developing their respective economic stimulus packages, and the overall global effort to stimulate the global economy was less effective because of this lack of cooperation and coordination (Petri and Plummer 2009).

As small economies, what Southeast Asian countries could contribute to a concerted global effort was obviously small. The region did deliver some significant fiscal packages in order to stimulate local growth (see Figure 1.4 of Chapter 1), including (commitment to fiscal stimulus in parentheses): Thailand (US$38.9 billion over three years); the Philippines ($6.7 billion); Indonesia (US$6.3 billion); and Malaysia (US$17 billion over two years). As expected, the larger packages (relative to GDP) were launched in the economies most affected by the crisis, i.e., Thailand and Malaysia. However, these packages were announced relatively late and some have complained that the actual disbursements have been significantly delayed. With the rise in economic growth globally, there will no doubt be a tendency to resist spending some/much of the rest ("time inconsistency" problem). Better preparation and planning would enhance the effectiveness of such fiscal policies in the future. Moreover, as ASEAN becomes more closely knit as a regional organization (discussed below), macroeconomic policy spillovers will become increasingly prominent, suggesting a role for closer cooperation and coordination in this area at the regional level.

With respect to monetary policies, the ASEAN countries exhibit significant differences in terms of their policy "anchors", for example: the Philippines uses an inflation target; Thailand, Indonesia and Vietnam use a mix of inflation and exchange rate targeting; and Malaysia keeps a fixed exchange rate (pegged to the U.S. dollar). Nevertheless, the foreign exchange anchor, particularly the U.S. dollar, seems to prevail. This is true even for the more flexible exchange rate regimes: according to Kim and Yang (2009), Southeast Asian (and Asian countries more generally) with greater flexibility in terms of their exchange rate regimes appear in practice to have less monetary policy freedom than those that do not. We noted above that this was also in evidence from recent changes in yield curves, which have generally followed U.S. trends.

The importance — and even dominance — of the U.S. dollar in the formation of monetary policy of Southeast Asia will likely fall over time, given changing trade structures, the rise of competing hard currencies (e.g., the euro), and, perhaps, the loss of confidence in the U.S. monetary and financial policies due to recent events. At the Fifteenth ASEAN Summit and ASEAN+3 heads-of-state meetings in Hua Hin, Thailand, end-October 2009, there was some discussion of how to reduce the dependence on the dollar, including the potential for a greater role for the Chinese RMB. Resisting revaluation of local currencies vis-à-vis the U.S. dollar prior to the crisis came at a significant cost, including the accumulation of foreign exchange reserves beyond what is optimal for the economy, higher interest rates and inflationary pressures, the bias in favour of net exports that has left the economies vulnerable (discussed above), and the bias against non-tradable goods. Hence, it will behove the Southeast Asian economies in the future to allow for greater flexibility vis-à-vis the U.S. dollar, perhaps via more appropriate policy baskets against which to peg local currency.

This will require more cooperation across the region. In particular, China is a major competitor of Southeast Asian economies in third markets, and the region will be loath to allow their currencies to appreciate if the Chinese RMB does not. This was one of the reasons for exchange rate misalignments prior to the ongoing crisis: some Southeast Asian countries no doubt would have preferred to revalue rather than to continue to have to sterilize major exchange rate interventions but did not because of a feared loss of competitiveness to China.[3] These problems are continuing even during this crisis. From March 2009 until end-October 2009, the RMB remained fixed to the dollar but the Thai baht and the Malaysian ringgit appreciated 7.7 per cent and 9.3 per cent, respectively.[4] While these appreciations are welcome in terms of "balancing" considerations, they are not likely to be sustainable unless the Chinese also allow the RMB to appreciate.

As a final point, to increase the effectiveness of aggregate demand management in developing Southeast Asian economies, it is important to improve financial markets, especially those related to fixed-income assets. Improving access to credit on the part of firms will provide another vehicle of investment for households, and help economies rebalance. Deepening financial and capital markets will also enhance the effectiveness of monetary policy and facilitate its implementation by, *inter alia*, lowering costs and bolstering liquidity. It will also improve fiscal policy and long-term public investments by lowering the cost of capital and reducing the potential for "crowding out".

Regional Economic Integration

Stimulating domestic demand in Southeast Asia is important, but this region will continue to be outward-oriented and improvements in international competitiveness will remain a top policy priority. Other growth engines will be needed, including in the Asian region itself. Indeed, a key motivation behind the myriad economic cooperation agreements that Southeast Asian economies have negotiated of late regards the need to improve the efficiency and attractiveness of the region's production networks as well as develop new markets for final demand. For Southeast Asia, ASEAN economic integration initiatives are being developed explicitly for these purposes, as well as to meet economic challenges from China and India in the global marketplace.

For example, the ASEAN Economic Community (AEC) programme, launched in 2007 and slated to be mostly complete in 2015, is by far the most comprehensive and ambitious effort by ASEAN to create a unified market. It aims to create free flows of trade in goods and services, a free flow of skilled labour and FDI, and a freer flow of capital. By eliminating obstacles to intra-regional trade and investment and the adoption of "best international practices", ASEAN hopes to enhance competitiveness of the region and position it to attract more production networks and FDI. Preliminary studies suggest that the potential effect will be large, with gains exceeding those of the EU Single Market Program.[5]

Still, intra-ASEAN trade is only just over one-fourth of the region's total trade and intra-regional FDI is even less than that (about 15 per cent): relations with the rest of the world are obviously extremely important to the region, with Asia taking up an increasingly important share of Southeast Asian trade and investment.[6] Hence, the AEC is explicitly outward-oriented, and the ASEAN member states have been active in negotiating free trade areas (FTAs) with their respective non-regional trading partners.[7] Many of these FTAs are now becoming ASEAN-centric (e.g., in the form of "ASEAN+1" agreements).

Such an approach to economic integration based on "open regionalism" and best practices should position the region well in the global marketplace and strengthen competitiveness at all levels. Nevertheless, as in the case of all deep integration programmes, it will take significant political commitment in order to achieve a single market by 2015 and create an ASEAN "hub" of FTAs over the next few years. This will pose significant leadership challenges.

Southeast Asian countries have also been active in creating an Asia-wide framework for financial and monetary cooperation. There are several other forums dealing with financial and monetary cooperation. The Executives' Meeting of the East Asia and Pacific Central Banks (EMEAP) is a forum of regional central banks; under it, the first Asian Bond Market Fund (ABF-1) initiative was launched in June 2003, followed in April 2004 by the ABF-2, which was created in 2005 and invested in local currency denominated bonds with initial seed money of US$2 billion. The ABF initiatives are managed under the auspices of the BIS and are funded through pools of reserves of the EMEAP central banks.

The ASEAN+3 Finance Ministers Meeting (ASEAN+3 FMM) and the APEC Finance Ministers Meeting process have also emerged in recent years. Established in the wake of the Asian crisis, the ASEAN+3 FMM focuses on financial sector cooperation, surveillance (including monitoring of capital flows), and policy dialogue. The "Chiang Mai Initiative" (CMI) was developed as part of the ASEAN+3 FMM. It began as a system of bilateral foreign exchange swap arrangements designed to support participating economies in case of a liquidity crisis, and in May 2009 was multilateralized and expanded to US$120 billion in resources. The Economic Review and Policy Dialogue (ERPD) was developed mainly to strengthen cooperation in the area of regional surveillance and foster dialogue on global, regional, and national economic developments. The APEC Finance Ministers' Meeting was first convened in 1994 and has now become a "process".

In short, Southeast Asia is participating in various financial and monetary initiatives but the current crisis demonstrates a greater need for cooperation and coordination. For example, an Asian Financial Security Dialogue (AFSD), which would include finance ministry and central bank officials, financial regulators and supervisors, and market participants, was proposed by ADB President Haruhiko Kuroda in September 2008. While the details of the AFSD have not yet been worked out, it could develop warning systems and surveillance mechanisms to improve the stability of the region's financial markets.

Keeping Existing and Attracting New Production Networks

The current crisis hit during a time of tremendous change in production processes, with global production networks driving rapid structural changes in trade patterns (ADB 2008). These networks have to no small degree been focused on supplying final goods to the U.S. market; the need to rebalance in the aftermath of the current crisis suggests that these production networks will need to diversify and reorient to new markets in Asia and Europe. To be competitive Southeast Asian economies will need to adapt to this emerging environment and prepare for even greater structural change.

The product mix in both exports and imports of Southeast Asian economies has changed significantly, from a bias towards natural resource intensive goods to a far greater dependence on electronics and other relatively sophisticated manufactures. Today machinery and transport equipment constitute about one-half of ASEAN exports and imports, up significantly since 1990. Indeed, manufacturing now account for almost three-fourths of total ASEAN exports, up from less than two-thirds in 1990.

Table 4.1 shows the top ten ASEAN exports and imports in 1990 and 2006. The change over time reflects, as expected, the rising significance of SITC 7 (machinery and transport equipment) in Southeast Asian trade. The biggest change has been the increase in importance of SITC 776 (thermionic valves) in both exports and imports. This product's export value has risen from US$12 billion in 1990 to US$120 billion in 2006, accounting for 16 per cent of total ASEAN exports of US$759 billion. ASEAN accounts for almost one-third of world exports of thermionic valves ($379 billion), which include: television picture tubes; other electrical valves and tubes; diodes, transistors, and similar semi-conductors; electronic microcircuits; and Piezo-electric crystals. In other words, exports of SITC 776 are parts of certain electronic value chains of which ASEAN forms the key link. The fact that imports of SITC 776 came to US$100 billion testifies to this.

In order to enhance growth prospects, ASEAN will need to maintain its advantage in this electronic value chain but also create additional ones, particularly as the global economy changes in the aftermath of the current crisis. Fragmentation of production — sometimes organized through a network of small, independent firms, more often by a big multinational corporation (MNC) that uses the region as a production base — is driven largely by technological change, but is also made possible by the low trade barriers and excellent transport and other links that make it cheap, quick and easy to ship goods within the region. Fragmented trade makes the most of each economy's various production advantages to boost productivity and cut costs, thereby rendering the economies more efficient and improving the standard of living via rising levels of technology. The AEC and various FTAs that the region and its constituent economies are forming should help in this process by lowering transactions costs associated with fragmented trade. Final demand for these products will also be increasingly geared towards Asian markets rather than the U.S. market.

Attracting FDI is obviously a necessary condition for greater participation in production networks, as well as in improving competitiveness in other tradable and non-tradable good sectors. In this regard, ASEAN's performance was more impressive prior to the Asian

TABLE 4.1
Top Ten Exports and Imports of ASEAN, 1990 and 2006

Exports (US$ billion)

1990		2006	
333-Petrol. oils & crude oils obt. from bitumin.	12.1	776-Thermionic, cold & photo-cathode valves, tub	119.6
334-Petroleum products, refined	11.5	334-Petroleum products, refined	47.4
776-Thermionic, cold & photo-cathode valves, tub	9.5	752-Automatic data processing machines & units	47.3
752-Automatic data processing machines & units	7.5	759-Parts of and accessories suitable for 751-	38.7
764-Telecommunications equipment and parts	6.2	333-Petrol. oils & crude oils obt. from bitumin.	32.3
341-Gas, natural and manufactured	6.0	764-Telecommunications equipment and parts	29.9
751-Office machines	4.2	341-Gas, natural and manufactured	20.9
232-Natural rubber latex; nat. rubber & sim. nat	3.8	931-Special transactions & commod., not class.t	16.0
931-Special transactions & commod., not class.t	3.7	772-Elect. app. such as switches, relays, fuses, pl	14.7
634-Veneers, plywood, improved or reconstituted	3.6	232-Natural rubber latex; nat. rubber & sim. nat	13.6

Imports (US$ billion)

1990		2006	
333-Petrol. oils & crude oils obt. from bitumin.	11.8	776-Thermionic, cold & photo-cathode valves, tub	109.9
776-Thermionic, cold & photo-cathode valves, tub	10.8	333-Petrol. oils & crude oils obt. from bitumin.	61.7
334-Petroleum products, refined	6.3	334-Petroleum products, refined	41.3
764-Telecommunications equipment and parts	6.2	759-Parts of and accessories suitable for 751-	28.2
792-Aircraft & associated equipment and parts	4.3	764-Telecommunications equipment and parts	25.0
728-Mach. & equipment specialized for particula	4.0	772-Elect. app. such as switches, relays, fuses, pl	15.0
751-Office machines	3.9	752-Automatic data processing machines & units	12.7
674-Universals, plates and sheets, of iron or st	3.7	778-Electrical machinery and apparatus, n.e.s.	12.4
931-Special transactions & commod., not class.t	3.2	792-Aircraft & associated equipment and parts	10.0
772-Elect. app. such as switches, relays, fuses, pl	2.9	728-Mach. & equipment specialized for particula	9.3

Source: UNCOMTRADE.

crisis than it has been since, with shares of global FDI falling from the general 7–8 per cent range prior to 1998 to about 4 per cent since (Table 4.2). Coupled with the fact that a disproportionate share of regional FDI (about 40 per cent) flows to Singapore alone, clearly attempts to lure greater FDI inflows are justified. The AEC attempts to combine "national treatment" of FDI in ASEAN with best practices, and most measures are ultimately non-discriminatory, that is, they do not favour ASEAN investors at the expense of non-ASEAN investors.[8] But much remains to be done in terms of microeconomic policy reform at the national level to significantly improve FDI inflows.

Microeconomic Policy Reform

As Southeast Asian economies rebalance as they emerge out of the crisis, they will need to not only maintain competitiveness in manufactured exports but also foster greater efficiency in local markets. Growth and development strategies in Southeast Asian economies have seriously neglected the non-tradable goods sector, particularly services, relative to the tradable sector. Remedying this bias will stimulate domestic demand and, in fact, improve the competitiveness of the tradable sector, given that, for example, services tend to be a critical input and facilitator of trade. Thus, a greater focus on services will have the dual benefit of strengthening domestic demand as part of the rebalancing process and improving competitiveness generally.

The World Bank's annual "Doing Business" rankings provide insight into the challenges ahead (Table 4.3). The ASEAN results in 2009 suggest the following:

- Southeast Asian economies differ widely in the ease of doing business, from a global ranking (of 181 economies) of 1 for Singapore to 165 for Lao PDR. Thailand, Malaysia, and Brunei have above average rankings, while the other ASEAN countries fall into the bottom half.
- Southeast Asian developing countries tend to rank poorly in the regulations for "starting a business" and (except Thailand and Singapore) for "registering property".
- ASEAN countries generally rank well in regulations affecting international trade (except for Cambodia and Lao PDR, with no information on Myanmar).

TABLE 4.2
World Shares of FDI Inflows to Selected Countries and Regions
(% Total World FDI Inflows, 1995–2006)

Year / Host	1995	1996	1997	1998	1999	2000	2001	2002	2003	2004	2005	2006	% of Cumulative Total (1995–2006)
United States	17.16	21.5	21.13	24.59	25.79	22.25	19.15	11.97	9.42	18.3	10.68	13.43	18.16
EU 25	38.3	31.8	29.1	39.6	45.7	49.3	45.8	49.4	45.5	27.5	51.4	40.7	42.8
Japan	0.01	0.06	0.66	0.45	1.16	0.59	0.75	1.49	1.12	1.05	0.29	–0.5	0.57
China	10.95	10.62	9.25	6.41	3.67	2.88	5.63	8.48	9.49	8.17	7.66	5.32	6.41
South Korea	0.36	0.51	0.54	0.72	0.9	0.64	0.5	0.55	0.78	1.21	0.75	0.38	0.66
East Asia	21.6	21.8	19.4	12.3	9.6	9.9	11.9	13.5	16.5	18.9	16.4	13.4	14.21
ASEAN	8.22	7.76	7.01	3.14	2.62	1.67	2.49	2.9	4.34	4.75	4.34	3.94	3.79
World (US$ million)	342,592	392,743	489,243	709,303	1,098,896	1,411,366	832,567	621,995	564,078	742,143	945,795	1,305,852	9,456,573

Notes: 1. The EU 25 includes: Austria, Belgium, Cyprus, the Czech Republic, Denmark, Estonia, Finland, France, Germany, Greece, Hungary, Ireland, Italy, Latvia, Lithuania, Luxembourg, Malta, the Netherlands, Poland, Portugal, Slovakia, Slovenia, Spain, Sweden, and the UK.
2. The figures for China do not include inflows to Hong Kong and Macao.
3. East Asia includes: China, Hong Kong, Lao PDR, Chinese Taipei, South Korea, Cambodia, Indonesia, Malaysia, Myanmar, the Philippines, Singapore, Thailand, and Vietnam.

Source: UNCTAD FDI Statistics Online.

TABLE 4.3
Ease of Doing Business in ASEAN
(Rank among 181 economies)

	Brunei	Cambodia	Indonesia	Lao PDR	Malaysia	Myanmar	Philippines	Singapore	Thailand	Vietnam	ASEAN Average
Ease of doing business	**88**	**135**	**129**	**165**	**20**	**N.A.**	**140**	**1**	**13**	**92**	**87**
Starting a business	130	169	171	92	75	N.A.	155	10	44	108	106
Dealing with construction permits	72	147	80	110	104	N.A.	105	2	12	67	78
Employing workers	5	134	157	85	48	N.A.	126	1	56	90	78
Registering property	177	108	107	159	81	N.A.	97	16	5	37	87
Getting credit	109	68	109	145	1	N.A.	123	5	68	43	75
Protecting investors	113	70	53	180	4	N.A.	126	2	11	170	81
Paying taxes	35	24	116	113	21	N.A.	129	5	82	140	74
Trading across borders	42	122	37	165	29	N.A.	58	1	10	67	59
Documents to export (number)	6	11	5	9	7	N.A.	8	4	4	6	7
Time to export (days)	28	22	21	50	18	N.A.	16	5	14	24	22
Cost to export (US$ per container)	630	732	704	1,860	450	N.A.	816	456	625	734	779
Documents to import (number)	6	11	6	10	7	N.A.	8	4	3	8	7
Time to import (days)	19	30	27	50	14	N.A.	16	3	13	23	22
Cost to import(US$ per container)	706	872	660	2,040	450	N.A.	819	439	795	901	854
Enforcing contracts	157	136	140	111	59	N.A.	114	14	25	42	89
Closing a business	35	181	139	181	54	N.A.	151	2	46	124	101

Source: Compiled from World Bank, Doing Business 2009.

Thus, the region has a long way to go in microeconomic policy reform. Singapore presents an excellent model of "best practices" to other countries in the region, which is important in terms of policy targeting. Still, improvement in these areas is notoriously difficult, as behind-the-border measures tend to face even greater political obstacles than border-related measures.

III. CONCLUSIONS AND RECOMMENDATIONS

The global economic crisis has severely affected Southeast Asian economies, though the extent of the damage differs significantly across them. The crisis has underscored many weaknesses in the international system of economic governance, and global "rebalancing" and improving international governance structures are arguably necessary conditions for stable, robust future growth. Hence, policy-makers will need to sustain their focus on forward-looking initiatives even as the political demand for change subsides.

This includes policy-makers in Southeast Asian countries. While "decoupling" (that is, less dependence on the OECD countries for economic growth) is in evidence to some degree, the current crisis has revealed that Southeast Asian countries continue to be significantly exposed to economic conditions in its traditional markets. We argue that there is much that Southeast Asian economies can do in order to rebalance their economies, rendering them less vulnerable to shocks of this nature, as well as increase competitiveness.

Despite the relatively small size of the region's economies, the fiscal expansion packages embraced by most ASEAN countries were appropriate; indeed relative to GDP they are larger than those of many European economies. Still, they were a bit late in coming and have been slow in being disbursed. Moreover, they were not undertaken in concert, whereas the closer integration of the ASEAN economies would suggest non-trivial externalities and that joint approaches would likely have yielded better results. Improved preparation and planning of stimulus packages in the case of global shocks, at the national and regional levels, would make good economic sense.

Rebalancing the global economy will be essential to the health of the Southeast Asian economies because of both the need for a prosperous international marketplace and for more balanced growth domestically. We have argued that countries can play their part by embracing more flexible exchange rate policies, reducing the bias towards net exports, improving productivity in the non-tradable sector (especially services), encouraging financial deepening, promulgating economic reform policies geared to improve fixed investment and consumption, and promoting investments in areas of long-run importance to economic growth and development, e.g., infrastructure and education.

Structural change in the post-crisis world will be increasingly led by the expansion of existing production networks and the creation of new ones. We identify a number of ways that Southeast Asia can bolster competitiveness in this regard, deeper economic integration at the ASEAN level through the AEC; FTAs with non-regional trading partners, including initiatives to keep ASEAN as the "hub" of action in Asia; adoption of economic reform and "best practices" in order to make the region more attractive to international and regional production chains and FDI more generally; and microeconomic reform. In addition, global initiatives such as a successful conclusion to the Doha Development Agenda talks, reform of international organizations such as the IMF, and improved regional institutions in Asia are essential to future regional growth. Investment in other "growth engines" will also be extremely important, particularly those related to the improvement in productivity (e.g., better secondary education in the transitional ASEAN economies, better universities and technical institutes in the ASEAN-6) and hard and soft infrastructure.

These recommendations will be difficult to implement and require significant political will. Hopefully the region will be able to harness the political momentum created by the crisis to launch these initiatives and set the foundations for sustained growth. We are confident that its leaders will do their best.

Notes

1. Singapore, which is also a member of ASEAN, is more open and is faring even worse. However, Singapore is a high-income, "advanced" economy and is included in Chapter 3. Thus, in this chapter we focus on the middle- and low-income ASEAN countries, but we occasionally do refer to Singapore.
2. As most Southeast Asian bond markets are not very liquid, the yield curve is less efficient in signalling risk in the market. However, the changes in the yield curve do reflect the policy choice to keep interest rates at certain levels.
3. The Thai government's decision in December 2006 to impose capital controls is a case in point. Contrary to the usual motivation, Thailand imposed capital

controls in order to slow the appreciation of the Thai baht (the results were not good, however, as the capital controls were greeted alarmingly by the markets).

4. A similar point is also made by Frangos (2009).

5. Plummer and Chia (2009).

6. ASEAN trade patterns are already changing significantly at present. Today, trade shares are relatively balanced between US/EU, Japan and China, and intra-ASEAN trade.

7. For a real-time update of these FTAs, see <www.aric.adb.org>.

8. Creating free flows of FDI in the AEC context is to be implemented through the ASEAN Comprehensive Investment Area (ACIA), formally adopted in 2009.

References

Adams, Charles. "Emerging East Asian Banking Systems 10 Years after the Asian Crisis". ADB Working Paper on Regional Economic Integration, No. 16, May 2008 <www.aric.adb.org>.

Asian Development (ADB). *Emerging Asian Regionalism*. Manila: ADB, 2008.

Cline, William. *The United States as a Debtor Nation*. Washington, D.C.: Institute for International Economics, 2005.

Frangos, Alex. "Yuan's Fall Annoys the Neighbors". *Wall Street Journal*, 26 October 2009. Available at <http://online.wsj.com/article/SB125650177290906749.html>.

Kim, Soyoung and Doo Yong Yang. "International Monetary Transmission and Exchange rate Regimes: Floaters vs. Non-Floaters in East Asia". ADBI Working Paper Series, No. 181, December 2009. Available at <http://www.adbi.org/files/2009.12.18.wp181.intl.money.trans.exchange.rate.regimes.pdf>.

McKinsey Global Institute. "The US Imbalancing Act: Can The Current Account Deficit Continue?". Mimeographed, June 2007.

Obstfeld, M. and K. Rogoff. "Global Current Account Imbalances and Exchange-rate Adjustments". *Brookings Papers on Economic Activity*, Vol. 1, edited by B. William and P. George (2005), pp. 67–46.

Petri, Peter A. and Michael G. Plummer. "The Triad in Crisis: What We Learned and What It Means for Global Economic Cooperation". *Journal of Asian Economics* (forthcoming).

Plummer, Michael G., and Chia Siow Yue. *Realizing the ASEAN Economic Community: A Comprehensive Assessment*. Singapore: Institute of Southeast Asian Studies, 2009.

5

North America: Achieving Sustained Growth

Wendy Dobson

I. HOW THE CRISIS AFFECTED NORTH AMERICA

The North American economy depends heavily on what happens in the United States. Canada and Mexico were negatively impacted by the decline in U.S. imports and rising unemployment but both countries had sound macroeconomic fundamentals. No Canadian financial firm failed and Canadian banks were rated as the world's soundest. In the United States, in contrast, the adjustments required in private and public saving and the consequent impact on real economic activity were widespread and large. The extent and timing of necessary financial regulatory reforms also contribute to considerable uncertainty about the path of a sustained recovery. The analysis that follows considers alternative scenarios and discusses five policy changes that would contribute to a sustainable outcome.

Sound macroeconomic positions in Canada and Mexico not only gave governments room to take aggressive recovery measures but each government also used the stimulus programmes to bring about structural changes to promote long-term growth. Both invested in physical infrastructure programmes and Canada expanded investments to upgrade its stock of human capital as part of the development of its knowledge-based economy. Although in 2009 Mexico suffered the largest contraction in real GDP among the emerging market economies (Table 5.1) both countries are expected to weather the recession successfully and to return to sustainable growth paths in 2010. This is apparent in the projected reductions in their structural fiscal deficits; the IMF expects that while Canada's fiscal deficit of –3.4 per cent of GDP in 2008 will extend into 2009 the underlying structural balance will be small (–0.9 and –0.8 per cent of GDP in 2009 and 2010, respectively). Mexico's fiscal balance was –1.4 and –0.3 per cent of GDP in 2008 and 2009, respectively, and will return to –0.4 per cent of GDP in 2010. It is also apparent in inflation projections; Canada's CPI inflation is expected to remain below 2 per cent while Mexico's is expected to remain in line with recent levels.

Uncertainties about U.S. prospects are expected to contribute to financial market volatility in the next few years unless credible actions are taken to restore large internal and external imbalances to sustainable positions. These have worsened as the administration fights the recession and foreign investors may lose confidence at some point in the future and refuse to finance further U.S. borrowing.

In the short term, economic activity appears to be stabilizing. Many forecasters expect real growth to return to 3 per cent by 2011 (Table 5.1) on the grounds that deep recessions are usually followed by sharp and fast recoveries. But this recession is atypical in that its causes lie in the financial sector where there is now a deep aversion to risk by both borrowers and lenders. Moreover, the macroeconomic policy response has been unprecedented and large adjustments will be required in both fiscal and monetary policies to restore them to sustainable long-term paths.

II. PROSPECTS FOR RECOVERY

There is thus considerable uncertainty about whether the recovery will be weak or whether organic growth will materialize more quickly than expected and the large stimulus package will not be withdrawn in time, igniting future inflation. Each concern has a credible basis. Withdrawal of stimulus too soon would nip recovery in the bud. The back-end loading of most public spending programmes means they will affect economic activity

TABLE 5.1
Real GDP, Consumer Prices and Current Account Balances,
Canada, Mexico, United States and China, 2008–2010

Economy	Real GDP (annual % change)				Consumer Prices (annual average change)			Current Acct Balance (% of GDP)		
	2008	2009	2010	2011	2008	2009	2010	2008	2009	2010
Canada (IMF)	0.4	−2.3	1.6		2.4	0	0.5	0.6	−0.9	−0.7
Mexico										
(IMF)	1.3	−7.3	3.0		5.1	4.8	3.4	−1.4	−2.5	−2.2
US										
IMF	1.1	−2.6	0.8	3.5	3.8	−0.9	−0.1	−4.7	−2.8	−2.8
OECD	1.1	−2.8	0.9					−4.7	−2.8	−2.4
Cline[1]										
(a)	1.1	−2.6	1.9	3.0				−4.7	−3.1	−4.5
(b)			1.9	3.0				−4.7	−3.1	−4.5
China										
IMF	9.0	7.5	8.5		5.9	0.7	0.1	10.0	10.3	9.3
ADB	9.0	7.0	8.0					10.1	8.4	7.8

Notes: 1. Cline presents alternative scenarios: (a) is the baseline scenario using current budget policy assumptions and numbers; (b) is the fiscal erosion scenario.
2. The Congressional Budget office projects real growth in 2010 to be 3.2 per cent while the Fed expects 2–3 per cent growth in 2010 and 3.5–4.8 per cent in 2011.

Sources: Real GDP from IMF (2009b); OECD Outlook and William Cline (2009); CPI and Current account balances from IMF (2009a), Chapter 2.

and jobs only in 2010 and 2011. This presents a difficult dilemma for the monetary authorities who must decide whether growth momentum in those years is organic or stimulus-driven. Unexpected strength of organic growth before monetary stimulus is withdrawn could be inflationary.

Prospects for Sustainable Fiscal Policy

The Congressional Budget Office (CBO) has evaluated the administration's plan to restore fiscal discipline. CBO estimates the federal fiscal deficit in 2009 will total 13 per cent of GDP compared to an historical average of between 2 and 3 per cent. The administration's plan is to reduce the deficit to 8 per cent of GDP in 2010, 5.9 per cent in 2011, 3.5 per cent in 2012 and reach plateau of 3.1 per cent in the 2013–19 period. But painful political decisions on taxation and spending will be required to realize these projections: tax cuts introduced in 2001 and 2003 which are due to expire after 2010 will have to be allowed to expire as required by current laws, and the alternative minimum tax (AMT), which is unindexed and will begin to hit middle income taxpayers in the years ahead, would have to be left unindexed. If these laws are observed and if spending is compressed in such programmes as defence, education, energy and other non-social spending categories room will exist for growth in social spending yet a sustainable deficit would be possible according to CBO, falling to 1 per cent of GDP in 2030.

These projections imply that the current account deficit which peaked in 2006 at 6 per cent of GDP will continue to decline, putting it at 3 per cent of GDP in 2010 (Table 5.1). But longer term projections by William Cline (2009) illustrate why optimism may be misplaced. He argues that the administration's sustainable fiscal deficit scenario described above is unrealistic because it will be politically impossible to compress spending on future non-entitlement programmes as the administration intends. This failure to achieve fiscal consolidation leads to an alternative "fiscal erosion" scenario. Cline assumes that, instead of reducing "other spending" sufficiently to make room for entitlement programmes, primary spending increases at a constant-share-of-GDP growth rate which causes it to rise continuously to 2030. He further assumes that the scheduled tax cuts do not expire and the AMT becomes indexed, both politically popular moves, which sees revenues unchanged as a share of GDP to 2030. As revenues fall behind spending, the impact of compound interest rates on debt servicing rises causing the fiscal deficit to reach 10.2 per cent of GDP by 2030. Without further changes in policy, the fiscal deficit will increase by 8 percentage points of GDP by 2030 over the 2–3 per cent that is generally accepted to be sustainable.

Cline uses a general equilibrium model to incorporate the relationship between the fiscal and trade deficits. He finds the change in the trade deficit is likely to be 40 per cent of the change in the fiscal deficit. The change in the current account is slightly larger. An important part of his arithmetic is his assumption that the dollar will rise through time, driven by the rise in long-term interest rates that accompany the rising deficit, which attract further capital inflows. In this fiscal erosion scenario, by 2030 exports are much lower because of the stronger dollar; net capital income is in deficit to the tune of 6.8 per cent of GDP driven by much larger net external liabilities, at 140 per cent of GDP. Because of the rise in the dollar, external assets are much smaller and liabilities are much larger reflecting the cumulative current account deficits and higher interest rates on the external debt. The long-term current account deficit will rise from 4.5 per cent of GDP by 2020 to 16–24 per cent by 2030. These are imbalances of sizes that "invite a crisis".

Will higher personal saving help to offset the borrowing effects? Cline argues that while personal saving rates will rise, corporate saving will decline (due to lower consumption, absence of stock market boom, etc.). Under the fiscal erosion scenario U.S. households will increasingly be transferring income to foreigners and will be forced to reduce their standard of living.

One could argue that the U.S. deficit and indebtedness will never reach such a size because markets will refuse to finance rising government borrowing and the dollar will depreciate, even "collapse", forcing U.S. policy-makers to raise taxes and cut spending in the midst of a new crisis. Either way, U.S. households are likely to have much less disposable income and public services unless the fiscal deficit is dealt with in a timely way. The value of Cline's analysis is to underline this point.

Prospects for Monetary Policy

Monetary policy conduct is also a major concern in any assessment of the prospects for a sustainable U.S. recovery. In the short-term the major concern of the Federal Reserve Board is to avoid a deflationary spiral as excess capacity puts downward pressure on prices, wages and spending. This outcome depends on the conduct of monetary policy: while it is quite likely that the Federal Reserve will err on the side of ease because of the economy's sensitivity to higher interest rates, investors are also highly sensitive to any signs that the central bank is printing money to finance the fiscal deficits. Inflation is unlikely to come from this source; instead, as recovery in demand takes hold, short-term interest rates will rise which will dampen inflationary pressures.

Both of these issues contribute to the "exit problem" as the major policy challenge facing U.S. policy-makers: how to time the withdrawal of fiscal and monetary stimulus without stifling market forces and prolonging or exacerbating the recession, on the one side, and without causing inflation on the other.

To avoid inflation in the medium-term, monetary policy must be tightened in a timely way and the Fed's balance sheet restored to normalcy. Monetary tightening could be politically controversial, as could measures to reduce the size of the Fed's balance sheet. Commercial banks have used the expanding money supply to restore and build up their reserves base rather than make new loans; as a result the size of the money multiplier in the United States (expected lagged impact on growth) has dropped significantly. As the financial system stabilizes, banks are expected to begin lending again; this is when the Fed should begin its exit, by drawing down the money supply and restoring its balance sheet to normal (at about a third of its size at the height of the crisis).

Alternative Scenarios

These policy challenges and uncertainties about the outlook contribute to alternative scenarios: one in which stimulus succeeds in restoring growth and the alternative where it fails.

Scenario A: Stimulus Succeeds in Restoring Growth

In Scenario A macroeconomic stimulus and financial sector reforms are adequate and sufficiently mutually-reinforcing that growth recovers and becomes self-sustaining. Most forecasters, particularly those in official organizations, currently subscribe to this scenario. They see the U.S. economy and the housing market stabilizing in the second or third quarter of 2009; financial institutions are also posting positive results which might suggest they have resolved their credit problems. Official forecasts put recovery beginning in early 2010 and U.S. growth returning to a long-term average of 3 per cent by 2011.

Scenario B: Stimulus Fails to Restore Growth

An alternative Scenario B is quite possible, however, in which growth is anaemic and in the extreme the economy falls back into recession by 2011. Many market analysts subscribe to this scenario for the following reasons: first, while consumption still accounts for 70 per cent of GDP consumers are only beginning to repair their balance sheets, helped along by tax breaks and other measures in the stimulus package. The savings rate is likely to continue to rise which will cut into disposable income; in addition, oil prices could rise and exacerbate the negative impact. Second, future credit conditions are uncertain. While a number of the largest banks have repaid Troubled Asset Relief Program funds and raised new capital, measures to remove toxic assets from bank balance sheets have been inadequate and many are thought to have retained these assets rather than accepting losses upon sale that would require them to add further to their capital bases. This reluctance could lead to further bad surprises in financial markets which would feed back into the real economy. Third, fiscal stimulus measures are flawed in two ways: they are proving slow to impact economic activity and many of the American Recovery and Reinvestment Act of 2009 expenditures were chosen by legislators to favour particular interest groups rather than being well-targeted measures that would save jobs or produce new ones. Further, in the absence of a credible plan to restore public finances to a sustainable course the public debt burden will rise along with rising long-term interest rates and rising debt servicing costs. Fourth, there are signs that as the unemployment rate rises, long-term structural unemployment is increasing because people are unable to find new jobs; structural unemployment will reduce economic potential in the years ahead as labour skills erode.

III. RESTORING SUSTAINABLE GROWTH

Scenario B highlights what is required for a sustainable North American recovery. First, U.S legislators must acquire the political will needed to restore U.S. fiscal policy to a sustainable track. They should speed up the impact of the stimulus measures and then begin fiscal consolidation, safeguard price stability and restore external balance. Cline's fiscal erosion path illustrates the risks inherent in Scenario B: a large increase in net external liabilities, rising debt servicing obligations and a lower standard of living. Clearly taxes will have to increase and/or spending will have to be cut.

Second, monetary policy faces the dilemma of timing its exit as growth picks up; if this growth is organic, exit will be successful, but if growth is still stimulus-driven tighter monetary policy will nip the recovery in the bud. The Fed, with pressure from financial markets, seems up to the task of avoiding inflation in the medium term, in light of the continued rise in unemployment and the increase in long-term unemployment. Governor Bernanke (2009b) has argued that the Fed will be able to reduce in a timely way liquidity in the system because much of its lending is short term; it can encourage banks to hold onto their reserves by offering them interest income to do so; it can conduct reverse repo agreements against its long-term securities to drain bank reserves. Thus, the necessary exit seems technically feasible, but politics are another matter. Monetary tightening will be required before the recovery has become established which will generate political backlash; the housing lobby could also resist the Fed selling its large mortgage holdings.

The other challenge in restoring sustainable monetary policy is to remove the unusual assets and liabilities on the Fed's balance sheet. It will have to find purchasers of the illiquid assets it acquired in the crisis in order to keep credit flowing that include lending to market participants in return for purchases of commercial paper and the provision of direct support to specific institutions such as emergency lending to facilitate the acquisition of Bear Stearns by JPMorgan Chase & Co. and to prevent AIG's default. Chairman Bernanke (2009a) insists the latter, higher-risk loans are expected to be repaid in full.

Third, regulatory policy poses another risk to sustainable growth. While the Treasury's proposed package of reforms includes the right measures, there is no clear agreement that their implementation would prevent another financial crisis or that they have removed moral hazard from the system (financial institutions taking more risk than they would if they were at the mercy of market forces for the full consequences of their decisions). Indeed, there are concerns that the government rescue has had the opposite effect. An additional concern is that toxic assets remain on bank balance sheets and the Public-Private Investment Program failed to provide the right incentives to deal with them. At the same time there are positive prospects for consolidating financial services oversight and more focus on systemic stability. But the authorities have not yet dealt decisively with the most troubling aspect of the crisis: the growing interconnectedness among internationally active financial institutions that are too big to fail. The financial institutions that are emerging from the crisis are fewer in number and financial power is becoming more concentrated in an oligopolistic structure in which incentives have been insufficiently changed to reduce risk taking.

The U.S. Treasury's preferred approach is to raise substantially the capital and liquidity requirements of all large financial institutions. Banking industry groups such as the Institute for International Finance caution against U.S. measures that prove to be inconsistent with European ones, such as the proposed U.S. requirements on capital and liquidity which are inconsistent with a proposed European approach in which leverage limits are more risk-based. Proposals to insulate tax payers from future bailouts of too-big-to-fail institutions also lack international consistency in that some governments call for an international bankruptcy regime and others such as the UK Treasury proposes to require such institutions to prepare their own plans to handle future insolvency in an orderly way. To avoid regulatory arbitrage, all significant regulatory authorities around the world should adopt similar standards and near-bank financial institutions should be subjected to such requirements.

Fourth, trade policy needs to support open markets. In response to criticism from the Canadian government and the European Union, the Obama administration refined the Buy America provisions to exclude all countries with which the United States has trade agreements but in September 2009 imposed a 35 per cent duty on automobile tyre imports from China, purportedly to gain union support for other initiatives. The Chinese government responded to both measures. As troubling as these measures are in the current environment, none contravened either domestic laws or provisions negotiated under the WTO during China's accession talks. Nevertheless the perception of a failure by the United States to refrain from protectionist measures sets an unfortunate example for other countries. Canada has been particularly vulnerable to the government procurement provisions which have affected Canadian producers despite the reinterpretation by the U.S. administration. On the bright side, the U.S. Trade Representative has indicated willingness to find ways to complete bilateral FTAs that have been negotiated but not ratified; however such initiatives are also being held in abeyance while the Administration focuses on health care reform. President Obama did, however, signal interest in other possible trade liberalizing initiatives, such as the Trans-Pacific Partnership (a comprehensive FTA which has been signed by Singapore, New Zealand, Chile and Brunei Darussalam, and which is open to other countries to join). The Free Trade Agreement of the Asia Pacific proposed for members of the Asia Pacific Economic Cooperation forum is currently in abeyance. Of course, the most powerful signal would be to reconvene and complete the Doha Development Round negotiations at the World Trade Organization.

Fifth, U.S. dependence on foreign central banks and investors to fund its current account deficit is the Achilles heel in this recovery. In particular, China and the United States must manage the symbiotic relationship in which China's excess savings finance excess U.S. consumption. For the United States, the major risk in this relationship is a collapse of the dollar should the Chinese sell their bond holdings on any large scale. This seems unlikely because losses would hit Chinese balance sheets as well. Instead, China is helping to stabilize the U.S. recovery by continuing to invest in U.S. government securities as long as it remains confident about the prospects for U.S. fiscal policy, inflation and growth. Americans can continue to expect to hear from its largest creditor about these concerns.

The challenge facing both governments is the composition and timing of measures to reduce the U.S. current account deficit and rebalance China's economy more towards domestic consumption. If the United States saves more and pays for its stimulus package rather than borrowing, the U.S. taxpayer faces higher taxes and spending cuts. China could allow yuan appreciation in order to reduce reliance on exports and increase the attractiveness of imports but a stronger yuan would make Chinese exporters less competitive at a time when they have already laid off millions of workers. Reduced investment in U.S. government securities would also cause U.S. interest rates to rise and threaten its recovery. Either way, both countries are in for changes which they would prefer be gradual and controlled. The most desirable path forward is that as the U.S. consumer saves more and spends less, China's exports decline and there will be fewer dollars to recycle. This assumes that China accepts the loss of exports and refrains from subsidies or measures to manage the exchange rate to make them artificially competitive. China will have to offset its export dependence by stimulating domestic demand — an inherent element of its rebalancing strategy. As consumption at home increases, Chinese would spend more and have less to lend to the United States. This is what will happen in the longer run, but it will take time to rebalance China's pattern of growth, raise consumer incomes and restore citizens' faith in publicly provided social services sufficient to increase consumption.

In summary, despite the promising signs of stabilization in 2009, North American recovery is likely to be weak and slow. A key signal that is needed in 2010 is a credible bipartisan initiative in the legislative branch to prepare a credible and enforceable plan for fiscal consolidation in the years ahead. In the absence of political will to restore sustainable fiscal policy, the task of monetary policy exit becomes more hazardous and the risks of an investor revolt rise. This leads to the question of whether there are potential changes that might be encouraged to provide new sources of dynamism necessary to grow out of the problem.

IV. ARE THERE POTENTIAL NEW GROWTH DRIVERS?

Are there potential new activities that could contribute to self-sustaining growth in the North American economy? In the short term these would be generated by government incentives and spending and by market forces as relative prices change during recession and recovery and in the longer term by entrepreneurs and investors identifying and exploiting new opportunities. Clearly, U.S. dollar depreciation will make major export sectors more price competitive in international markets. Major export sectors include aircraft, integrated circuits, capital equipment, parts and components and metals such as copper and aluminum as well as agricultural commodities such as soy beans and cotton — and commercial services such as travel, transportation, business and financial services. As well, royalties and licence fees accounted for nearly 17 per cent of total exports in 2007.

Government incentives and public sector spending have affected short-term demand. Recovery Act expenditures have assisted state governments to fund physical infrastructure and other public projects that have saved jobs from being lost; because of the delay in the injection of this spending into the economy, new jobs will only be created in 2010 and 2011. The Obama administration also identified green growth initiatives to encourage the expansion of renewable and cleaner energy supplies, the automation of medical records and expansion of health care services, and new sources of revenue from auctioning carbon permits in the proposed cap and trade system to reduce greenhouse gases. Unfortunately, however, the short-term impacts of such initiatives have been substantially weakened in the legislative process as legislators respond to influential interest groups who benefit from the status quo.

There is a deep aversion in U.S. policy towards "industrial policies" and a greater reliance on the drivers of long-term output growth. These include changes in labour force quality through education and immigration and changes in labour supply through demographic changes such as population ageing. Other sources are better mobilization and allocation of financial capital, discovery of new natural resources, and technological changes. Population ageing will increase demand for health care and other services for the foreseeable future. Financial reforms that reduce risk taking by the largest financial institutions may open avenues for growth of new, less risky but profitable commercial banks in the United States. In the energy sector access to abundant new supplies of natural gas deposited in shale formations throughout North America are beginning to impact economic activity and jobs and to put downward pressure on natural gas prices in Canada and the United States. Entrepreneurs have also responded to the rising popularity of green goods and services. Wind and solar power sources, while small in their total contribution to overall electricity demand, have already generated "green collar jobs" among suppliers of equipment and construction services.

Finally, it would be a mistake to underestimate the inherent dynamism of American economic institutions. To the extent businesses throughout the economy — in manufacturing industries such as advanced materials, semi-conductors and computing, energy, electrical displays, the auto industry, and in sophisticated services — improve their capabilities through innovation and investments in basic and applied research, their dynamism will continue as it has in the past to contribute to North America's productivity growth.

References

Bernanke, Ben. "The Federal Reserve's Balance Sheet". Remarks at the Federal Reserve Bank of Richmond 2009 Credit Markets Symposium, Charlotte North Carolina, 3 April 2009*a*.

———. "Regulatory Restructuring". Testimony before the Committee on Financial Services, U.S. House of Representatives, Washington, D.C., 24 July 2009*b*.

Cline, William. "Long-Term Fiscal Imbalances, US External Liabilities, and Future Living Standards". In *The Long-Term International Economic Position of the United States*, edited by C. Fred Bergsten. Special Report 20. Washington, D.C.: Peterson Institution for International Economics, May 2009.

International Monetary Fund. "World Economic Outlook". April 2009*a*.

———. "World Economic Outlook Update". July 2009*b*.

United States Treasury. "Financial Regulatory Reform: A New Foundation", 17 June 2009.

6

South America:
Achieving Sustained Growth

Raimundo Soto

I. HOW THE CRISIS AFFECTED SOUTH AMERICA

South American countries have a long, infamous tradition of suffering economic crisis. Nevertheless, the current global crisis is radically different from previous episodes in its genesis, its impacts and its most likely evolution. This paper studies the effect of the crisis in four South America economies that are members of the PECC (Chile, Colombia, Ecuador, and Peru, henceforth called South America) and the policy responses by monetary and fiscal authorities. The storyline can be summarized in five simple conclusions: (a) this crisis was externally driven; (b) South America has had good preconditions and policy space to weather the crisis and used it reasonably well (except for Ecuador); (c) the recovery is underway and, in fact, better than in more advanced economies (North America and Europe); (d) however, the region is too small to determine its own macroeconomic prospects; but (e) there are several policies it can do to keep its credibility and finances intact.

This economic downturn did not start at home; South American economies have been casualties of the "toxic assets" crisis and the poor response of policy-makers in the United States and Europe. Contrary to local traditions, this crisis has not been accompanied by financial sector turmoil or collapses in the balance of payments, nor has it caused apparent damage to the financial sectors beyond the expected credit tightening of any cyclical downturn. The crisis has been largely confined to the real sector, in particular to foreign trade. At this writing, it also appears that the aftermath of the crisis will not be as severe as in some previous cycles. An early recovery seems to be at hand, at least for the most advanced regional economies.

As discussed below, three of the four South American economies were better prepared to face the crisis than had been the regional norm in previous downturns. Consequently, they have managed to escape the adverse shock relatively unharmed, due to a combination of years of prudent fiscal policy, sound banking systems, low foreign indebtedness, and massive international reserves. There have been no financial crashes, nor balance of payments crisis or runs against local currencies, even in countries experiencing capital flows reversals. In contrast, Ecuador is a dollarized economy that has been unable to overcome most of the weaknesses that plagued South American countries decades ago and, consequently, has paid — and will continue to pay — a substantial welfare cost due to its poor policy responses to the crisis.

Transmission Channels

The economic crisis spread through different channels and with varying intensity. First, the crisis in the United States led to widespread uncertainty and collapses in asset values. Projections for the world economy became progressively more uncertain and as confidence in policy-makers in industrial countries shrunk, uncertainty skyrocketed. Following the trend, asset values collapsed in the South American PECC countries during the second half of 2008 (see Figure 1.2 in Chapter 1); stock market prices declined by 10–15 per cent in Chile and Colombia in the third quarter of 2008 with respect to December 2007 and by 36 per cent in Peru. Then, in the last quarter they plunged again, leading to annual losses of 22 per cent in Chile, 29 per cent in Colombia, and 60 per cent in Peru.

The second transmission channel was the reversal of capital flows and the increase in financing costs. Increased uncertainty in world financial markets led to a sharp increase in the cost of access to international financial markets. Although interest rates declined throughout the industrial world, country risk premium for South American PECC economies doubled between September and November 2008. Ecuador *de facto* defaulted on its external obligations by the end of 2008, losing all access to external financing.

The third and most important transmission channel was the collapse of foreign trade, the result of sharp reductions in both the volume and price of exports (Figure 1.2). By the end of 2008, import volumes in OECD countries had contracted by about one-third from their peak in July. In Colombia, Ecuador and Peru, the trade collapse was deepened by the concentration of exports in U.S. markets, while Chile benefited from having a more diversified exports. Idiosyncratic factors at the country level also affected exports negatively.

A fourth channel involved a massive decline in commodity prices. The extremely high prices observed until mid-2008 make the decline look more dramatic than it actually was, for authorities and economic agents anticipated that the price windfall would not last. However, in terms of current fiscal revenues, foreign currency availability and expectations, the decline in commodity prices was still very significant. While export prices dropped markedly, import prices declined: oil prices fell by two-thirds by the end of 2008, damaging oil producers (Ecuador) but benefiting oil importers (Chile). Nevertheless, terms of trade have declined between 20 per cent and 25 per cent between mid-2008 and June 2009 for the four South American PECC countries.

The fifth transmission channel was the drop in workers remittances (resources sent home by individuals working overseas), especially from those residing in the United States, but also across South American countries. Remittances are negligible in Chile, but they are significant in Colombia and Peru and very important in Ecuador. In July 2009, the World Bank forecast a decline of around 10 per cent in remittances for 2009, which translates into a foreign transfer loss of 0.3 per cent of GDP in Colombia and Peru and 0.8 per cent of GDP in Ecuador.

Impact of the Crisis

Prior to the crisis, South America enjoyed a period of an unprecedented expansion, reducing poverty and improving income distribution. Despite the region's better grounding, countries will not escape unscathed from the crisis. According to ECLAC (2009a), as a result of the crisis GDP in South American economies will fall on average by around 2 per cent in 2009, indicating a contraction in GDP growth of around 6 percentage points from the previous five-year average. Chile, a very open economy that relies on exports to sustain growth, will see a decline in GDP of around 1 per cent. Colombia will decline as well. Peru, the rising regional star, will continue to benefit from recent, substantial structural reforms and will manage to keep positive growth, but will see it slowdown markedly to 2 per cent. Ecuador's economy will crash with a 3.2 per cent contraction in GDP.

Although these outcomes are severe, given the adverse global environment they could have been worse. South America was better prepared for the global crisis than in the past. Lessons painfully learned during the 1980s and 1990s led policy-makers to enact strict financial regulations (which proved instrumental in avoiding financial panics in this crisis), reduce external debts and accumulate massive foreign reserves (providing insurance "for the rainy day" and inhibiting runs against the currency), and streamline fiscal policies (raising credibility and providing space for the authorities to implement counter-cyclical policies). In Chile, Colombia, and Peru central banks operate under inflation-targeting schemes and policy-makers enjoy high credibility. Chile implemented a "fiscal expenditures rule" committing itself to maintain a long-run fiscal surplus of 0.5 per cent of GDP and forcing itself to save abroad most of the copper price windfall of recent years (to the tune of 15 per cent of GDP).

Lessons, however painful, have not been learned in all economies. Ecuador achieved macroeconomic stability after dollarizing in 2002, but continuous fiscal mismanagement, protectionism, political interference, and rampant corruption have nearly destroyed the internal credibility in economic authorities and defaulting on the foreign debt last December destroyed any access to international financial markets in the midst of the downturn.

Aside from declining export volumes, the impact of the crisis reflects in shrinking investment and a substantial slowdown in private consumption. This is the inevitable result of weakening confidence on South American economies quickly overcoming the crisis. In addition to gloomy perspectives, investment falls are expected as a result of the 40 per cent decline in foreign direct investment (FDI). Private consumption drops will be significant in Chile and Ecuador (reflecting the 10 per cent fall in remittances) but less so in the other economies. Public consumption, on the other hand, quickened in most economies (5 per cent on average, year-on-year) in part as a result of active counter-cyclical policies and also due to improved revenue collection from high commodity prices. Since elections are to be held in Chile, Colombia and Peru by the end of 2009, the political cycle might also contribute to the fiscal expansion.

II. MACROECONOMIC POLICIES IN THE CRISIS

The pre-crisis situation was very favourable for counter-cyclical policies in three South American-PECC countries (Chile, Colombia, and Peru), allowing ample space for coordinating monetary, exchange rate, and fiscal policies. Because financial integration in the sub-region is relatively high, monetary and exchange rate policies are not truly independent (as indicated by Mundell's "impossible trinity" argument). In the past, some South American PECC countries have chosen to de-link from world markets in the face of a major crisis, closing their capital account to regain monetary policy independence. However, the long-run benefits of financial integration are judged to be worth its short-run costs. Recent experience confirms the high costs of de-linking; in 2008 Ecuador tried to impede capital flows by administrative measures, only to see country risk skyrocket and credibility wane, losing all access to much-needed financial resources from foreign sources.

Policy Constraints

Several major constraints have limited the scope of expansionary policies in the South American-PECC countries (Fernández-Arias and Montiel 2009). The first limitation arises from the monetary regime: two of the economies studied do not have an independent monetary policy because they have dollarized (Ecuador) or maintained a *de facto* fixed exchange rate (Peru), while the other countries conduct monetary policy within inflation-targeting schemes where the credibility of the Central Bank is a key determinant to success. Prior to the crisis, countries maintained a tight monetary stance to control the inflation upsurge that came along with the rise in international commodity prices in early 2008. Inflation receded by mid-year following the sharp plunge in world prices for food and fuels and as a result of the toll taken by the global crisis on domestic demand.

The rapid decline in inflation led to relatively high ex-post interest rates which further depressed aggregate demand, particularly in Chile and Colombia that were reluctant to reduce policy interest rates fearing the loss of their hard-earned credibility. As the global economy cooled off, swift adjustments by Central Banks led interest rates to historical lows in Chile, Ecuador, and Peru. By May 2009 average annual inflation in South American PECC economies was a mere 2.0 per cent. Thus, the space for counter-cyclical monetary policies was rapidly used to enact an aggressive reduction in policy interest rates.

The pre-crisis external stance also provided space for policy (except in Ecuador). First, massive foreign reserves and low post-crisis import levels allow using reserves to finance expansionary policies. Second, low external debts indicate unused borrowing capacity. In particular, public debts are at historical lows ranging from 12 per cent of GDP in Chile to 30 per cent in Colombia. As a result of the crisis, trade surpluses narrowed, current transfers shrank, remittances declined and the current account deteriorated in 2008–09 with an average deficit of 3.5 per cent of GDP. While financing these deficits does not seem to be problematic, these favourable external conditions do not automatically translate into easy access to foreign financing, as indicated by the relatively high risk premium on sovereign debts (EMBI spreads range from 100 pp in Chile to 350 in Colombia and Peru).

A second potential constraint to counter-cyclical policies is that of currency mismatch leading to balance-sheet effects. It may not be possible to rely on exchange rate depreciation to sustain the demand for domestic goods when there is "fear of floating" and, in particular, when currency mismatch poses a serious danger for the financial sector (Calvo and Reinhardt 2002). In Chile and Colombia this may not be a serious constraint, because financial regulation is designed to avoid currency mismatch (a lesson learned during the Debt Crisis of 1982). On the contrary, the *de facto* fixed exchange rate of Peru and the high degree of informal dollarization indicate some risks of engineering a devaluation to boost domestic demand. In Ecuador de-dollarization could lead to the total collapse of the financial sector and be devastating for producers.

Finally, the fiscal stance was also favourable for counter-cyclical policies although with some important limitations. Fiscal expansions are effective only to the extent that they are credible. If agents anticipate that the fiscal stance is unsustainable, they will increase saving to cover themselves for the moment when taxes will be raised in the future to pay current deficit. In addition, expansionary fiscal packages may trigger a harmful increase in default risk spreads, especially if initial debt levels are high relative to a government's debt-servicing capacity as in Ecuador. The initial situation in the sub-region was mixed. Large fiscal surpluses were recorded in 2008 in Chile (5.3 per cent of GDP) and Peru (2.2 per cent), suggesting ample space for counter-cyclical policies. Significant fiscal deficits in Colombia (2.2 per cent) and Ecuador (1.2 per cent) suggested the opposite situation.

However, sustainability and solvency concerns may severely constrain available counter-cyclical policies. Expansionary policies imply larger fiscal deficits and, when financed by higher public debt, they may increase the perception of government insolvency. If financed by foreign reserves, they may increase government vulnerability to liquidity crunches and sudden stops in lending. Both intensify the fiscal sustainability challenge. Including a measure of unused borrowing capacity, Izquierdo and Talvi (2008) estimate that there was ample room for sustainable fiscal expansions in Chile, Colombia, and Peru at the onset of the crisis. The report excludes Ecuador, but one can safely conclude that fiscal space for expansionary policies is largely unavailable.

Actual Policy Responses

The policy response has taken several forms that can be grouped in (a) those aimed at restoring confidence and grease financial markets and (b) those aimed at strengthening domestic demand (ECLAC 2009b). A summary description of policies is presented in Tables 6.1 and 6.2. At the onset of the crisis, policies comprised almost exclusively central banks providing liquidity to financial markets to normalize operations, securing access to credit and lowering financial costs to reasonable levels. These were mostly "confidence restoration" policies. Nevertheless, lower interest rates and improved access to funds did not automatically translate into credit expansion, both because banks become more conservative when offering credits and families likewise hesitate to expand their demand. These led to additional measures aimed at expanding credit to the private sector and, later, to announcing and partially implementing ambitious proposals for fiscal expansions.

Expansionary monetary policy led interest rates close to zero. In some countries, quantitative easing procedures have gone to the point of having

TABLE 6.1
Monetary and Financial Policy Responses to the Crisis

Policies	Chile	Colombia	Ecuador	Peru
Monetary policy	Policy interest rate lowered from 8.25% in January 2009 to 0.75% in July.	Policy interest rate lowered from 10% in December 2008 to 5% in June 2009.	Central Bank suspends a preannounced reduction of interest rates until June 2009.	Policy interest rate lowered from 6.25% in February 2009 to 4% in May.
	Provision of liquidity in foreign currency (currency swaps).	Provision of liquidity in foreign currency on a discretionary basis.	Provision of liquidity in foreign currency by extend tax credits (12.5% of new financial resources allocated to productive investment).	Provision of liquidity in foreign currency (extending repayment of loans granted by Central Bank to private sector) and swap operations.
	Provision of liquidity in domestic currency (repo operations).	Provision of liquidity in domestic currency (repo operations).	Delaying repayment of interest on public debt and forcing conversion to new debt.	Provision of liquidity in domestic currency (repo operations up to one-year maturity).
Financial system interventions	Flexibilization of reserve requirements for financial institutions.	Flexibilization of reserve requirements for checking and saving accounts.	Imposing taxes on idle resources held overseas by private financial institutions. Tax on capital outflows raised from 0.5% to 1%.	Flexibilization of reserve requirements for domestic and foreign currency (5 adjustments between end 2008 and mid 2009).

Tax adjustments to expand demand of public bonds, subsidies to refinancing of SMEs, increased access to factoring, State guarantees for loan restructuring.	Elimination of capital controls on portfolio investment and foreign direct investment.	Delaying repayment of interest on public debt and forcing conversion to new debt. De facto default.
	Elimination of reserve requirements for overseas investment (by Colombians).	Credit lines for banks and financial institutions by the State Bank (Banco Nacional de Fomento).
		Social Security forced to buy mortgages held by private banks against the banks' promise to lend these resources to housing projects on the terms and conditions prevailing in 2008.

TABLE 6.2
Fiscal Policy Responses to the Crisis

Chile	Colombia	Ecuador	Peru
Fiscal stimulus plan (US$4 billion or 2.8% of GDP).	Fiscal stimulus plan (US$3.8 billion or 4% of GDP).	No plan, but isolated measures announced.	Fiscal stimulus plan (US$4 billion or 3.2% of GDP).
Expenditures to grow around 2.5% of GDP, 70% in social programs. Infrastructure expand mostly in public works (35%), housing (15%); health (5%); and support for SME (16%).	Prioritizes public expenditure on roads, housing, water and sanitation, irrigation and social programs, exports support plan.	Granting loans to public officers to impulse domestic demand, granting banks access to fiscal support against allocating resources to loan to selected sectors.	Resources allocated to infrastructure (30%), support non-traditional exporters, SMEs and workers (10%), improving social protection networks (10%) and paying State overdue bills to oil refining companies (25%).
Financing comes from fund that collected public saving from the commodity price boom.	Financing comes from a mix of government reserves and loans from multinational organizations.	Financing would come from negotiating loan from IADB to cover fiscal expenditures.	
Other financing will come from issuing public debt and a transitory reduction in the fiscal rule surplus.		Additional financing from subsidies cuts for PetroEcuador.	Government issues bonds to finance 2010 budget.
Lowering taxes for SMEs and corporations, increased and new (targeted) subsidies and new tax benefits.	Lowering taxes for SMEs and corporations, increased and new (targeted) subsidies and new tax benefits.	Lowering taxes for exporters and banks, and postponing tax payments for firms and businesses.	Increased export drawback from 5% to 8% for non-traditional exporters.

Overdue taxes horizon extended to three years before seizing of assets.	Lowering payroll taxes for newborn SMEs for three years.	Comprehensive tax-reform proposals (not passed as law yet).	Fund to provide state collaterals for private sector investment.
Transitory raise on housing subsidies for poor and middle class households.	Housing program and subsidizing interest rates charged on housing loans.	Raising tariffs (to 35%) and imposing quota restrictions on consumption goods.	
Capitalization of the state bank to expand credit to SMEs.	Credit line to finance purchase of cars and support the assembly factories in Colombia.	Lowering import duties for capital goods and raw materials not domestically produced.	Direct transfer to consumers to finance purchase of new cars and retire old, damaged units.
State collaterals for new, private sector investment.	Cooperation agreement between Colombia and Spain for investments.		
Forestry sector tax-incentives extended.		Expediting the payment of export drawbacks and exemption/delay from paying income taxes.	
Bail-out salmon industry.			
Capitalization of Copper State Corporation.	New credit lines for exports and imports.		

central banks providing financial intermediation and even direct lending to manufacturing enterprises, and eventually recapitalization of financial institutions. Fiscal policies are based on the notions that increased expenditures have more short-term impact than tax reductions, that direct transfers have more impact than other expenditures but are harder to implement and target, and that public investment in infrastructure has biggest impact on economic activity and employment. All four economies announced "crisis recovery plans": in Chile, Colombia, and Peru these plans are sizeable (between 2.8 per cent and 4.2 per cent of GDP), their financing is sustainable, but their content is quite heterogeneous and their possible impact still uncertain, as discussed below. These plans include massive investment in infrastructure, support for SME, direct and targeted transfers to poor households, and transitory cuts in taxes. Ecuador's fiscal stimulus plan corresponds to the old fashioned interventionist approach to crisis, with government resorting to administrative and arbitrary measures such as defaulting on the external and internal debt, intervening financial markets, sequestering household savings in pension funds to finance current expenditures, and engaging in protectionist trade practices, even against countries with which it had preferential trade agreements.

It is too early to properly evaluate these policies as the crisis is still unfolding. The policy response in Chile, Colombia, and Peru to the very deep contraction in aggregate demand is similar to that of industrial countries or emerging economies in East Asia. However, the source of the problems is not the same. The shock, so far, has not led to domestic financial distress; the financial sector component of stimulus plans is then hard to justify. Also, the effectiveness of counter-cyclical policies — particularly fiscal policy — may be limited in the very open South American PECC economies if it only leads to additional spending on foreign goods.

The main issue is, nevertheless, on the timing of policies. Monetary policy responded too little in the onset of the crisis and too much at the peak. Initially, central banks did not adjust policy interest rates fast enough in view of the fast falling inflation rates, leading to a period of high real interest rates and credit costs, deepening the downturn. More recently, they lowered policy interest rates very aggressively, perhaps too late to counteract its initial indecision and re-build credibility. Of course, the counter-factual is difficult to pinpoint and real-time decisions are much more difficult to make than what ex-post analysis indicate.

With regards to fiscal policies, the emphasis on infrastructure might be justified on a long-run development basis, although the impact of public investment in boosting the domestic demand will take time to materialize. Other support measures are better targeted and should have an impact on households (transfers and housing subsidies) and SMEs which, being labour intensive, help reduce unemployment. Nevertheless, when providing such boost to public expenditures, the quality of social programmes and the social profitability of investment tend to decline markedly.

III. WHAT ARE THE PROSPECTS FOR RECOVERY?

The South American PECC economies are poised to return to growth. Reasons for optimism include the region's healthy financial systems (improved regulation and supervision, and absence of "toxic assets"), relatively strong central banks that are able to implement credible monetary policies, flexible exchange rate arrangements (in Chile and Colombia) that provide an automatic stabilizer for external financial shocks, and effective fiscal systems that allow flexibility and encourage responsibility. Reforms in the 1990s may have left the region more exposed to external shocks but they also made economies more resilient.

Nevertheless, this outlook is subject to major risks. First, since the four economies are small and open, their recovery depends to a large extent on the fate of developed economies. Consensus growth projections for the South American PECC economies indicate a recovery of activity by the end of 2009 and a strong upswing in 2010. The region's optimistic forecasts are based on a relatively fast recovery of economic activity in the industrial world and, in particular in China which has become the region's main trading partner (trade between South America and China rocketed from US$10 billion in 2000 to US$140 billion in 2008). The IMF is projecting China's growth to reach 8 per cent in 2009 and higher rate in 2010. Should this falter, recovery in the four economies would be very slow.

Second, should the global crisis be prolonged, financing large current account deficits could prove difficult, even though countries entered the crisis with substantial foreign exchange reserves. This risk seems to be receding since by the second quarter of 2009 countries regained access to international capital markets.

Third, industrial countries could resort to protectionism as a mechanism to boost domestic demand. This, of course, would hurt recovery in South America, affecting the more open economies the most. It is true, though, that protection tends to be used more often to block the entry of manufactured goods (of the sort exported by East Asia) than to natural resources and services (of the sort exported by other emerging economies).

Fourth, the recovery in trade might not be matched by a recovery in financial markets. If international and domestic markets remain tight for some time, the ability of exporters to invest and capitalize on faster growth could be hurt. This risk is compounded with that arising from the political cycle. Elections in Chile and Colombia and turmoil in Peru might lead entrepreneurs to postpone investment and risk taking.

Finally, the region's public debt is rising. According to the IADB, even if world recovery is rapid the public debt in South American PECC economies will increase from 27 per cent of GDP in 2008 to 34 per cent from 2010. But if world recovery falters, governments will have to borrow more every year, which would take the average debt ratio to around 50 per cent of GDP in four years. This scenario could trigger a liquidity crisis, if an economy does not have sufficient international reserves to cover the service of the external debt. That possibility seems remote in view of the high levels of reserves held by countries, but IABD calculations show that four years is long enough for a liquidity crisis to break out in almost any economy in which the government and the corporate sector have to refinance their short-term debts, as is already beginning to happen.

IV. TOWARDS SUSTAINED GROWTH

Even if the short-term risks are avoided, substantial reforms will be needed to strengthen productivity. Pro-market reforms initiated in Chile in the 1980s and in Colombia and Peru in the 2000s liberalized domestic and external markets which allowed fast growth, largely supported by private investment directed to the extraction of natural resources and the use of abundant unskilled labour. However, the limits to this intensive factor-accumulation strategy are becoming evident, indicating the need to implement swift policy changes. Total factor productivity in the last twenty years has grown at meagre rate of 1 per cent per year, very low in comparison to the 2.5 per cent of Asian tigers.

Productivity is an encompassing term, comprising technology adoption, human capital development and the efficiency of the State in providing public goods and infrastructure. In all South American PECC economies there is an evident need for policies fostering technology innovation and adoption, along with the reinforcement of intellectual property rights. Expenditures in R&D are 0.7 per cent of GDP in Chile and a meagre 0.2 per cent in Colombia, Ecuador and Peru, against 2.5 per cent in the United States (ECLAC 2009c). Possible engines for long-run growth in this area relate to the development of non-traditional technology-intensive exports (e.g., the wine industry in Chile) and the implementation of cost-saving projects in energy, transportation, and telecommunications. Human capital formation, on the other hand, has been invoked as a key to sustained growth by authorities in all countries, yet progress in the last decade is negligible. In Chile, private sector initiatives have led to substantial increases in coverage and access to education, yet quality has not progressed accordingly. Outdated, top-down education policies in Chile, Peru and Colombia are a major deterrence to sustained growth. Finally, in the four South American PECC economies the state is the main limitation to sustained long-run economic growth. Public services such as health, education, or housing are generally provided by the state very inefficiently, untimely, and at a high cost to the population. While lack of resources is usually the culprit, it is obvious that poor management, corruption, and political interference are at the roots of the problems. Public sector reforms, however difficult, hold the promise of higher productivity and better quality of life for the population.

External risks are the main concern for recovery in the short run. Lack of reforms is the main restriction to sustained growth. There are two key challenges to maintaining growth in the mid-term. First, removing the distorting measures embedded in current stimulus plans, withstanding the pressure of interest groups and political parties to keep preferential treatments. Recovery plans include distorting measures aimed at supporting specific sectors, tax cuts, increased transfers and the like, which need to be removed once the crisis is over to re-align incentives. Beneficiaries of preferential policies will manoeuvre to keep their privileges long after the crisis is over; political parties are often captured by interest groups. These policies, however, damage productivity and long-run growth for two reasons: protection inhibits inefficient producers to exit the market and, while keeping them in the market, inhibit the entry of most productive producers, thus hampering productivity growth.

Second, the current development strategy will likely be critically evaluated after the crisis, in particular to identify weaknesses and vulnerabilities. While major policy changes are unlikely in the short to medium term, measures to reduce vulnerability to foreign shocks should be considered. On this, several proposals have been advanced. First, diversifying trade partners would provide cushioning against adverse trade shocks as long as they are not global. Chile, and more recently Peru, achieved a substantial diversification by signing free trade agreements. Second, diversifying the export base would hedge against commodity price shocks to which South American PECC economies are particularly vulnerable. Support for non-traditional exports and developing services seem to be crucial for risk diversification; in particular, tourism is an area that, if properly developed, could provide a boost to sustained economic growth in the four countries.

Additional macroeconomic policies could further reduce the risks. While exchange-rate flexibility is necessary for an efficient allocation of resources, it also tends to increase currency uncertainty; hence, authorities should develop insurance mechanisms along two lines. One strategy is to encourage the financial sector to develop new coverage and financing instruments (such as forwards, options, derivatives, and venture capital markets) and provide the adequate regulation to minimize systemic risks. A second strategy is to reduce the impact of macroeconomic fluctuations on exchange rates. Stabilization funds for commodity price dependent economies such as Chile proved to be crucial to avoid the harmful effects of the price cycle, by forcing the government to save extraordinary earnings for the rainy day. Forcing fiscal budgets to be intertemporally consistent (e.g., fiscal rules) seem to be an additional tool to smooth out government expenditures and cushion the economy against external fluctuations filtering through government spending. Both stabilization funds and fiscal rules also serve the purpose of isolating the conduct of fiscal policy from the political cycle, which has been pervasive in South American countries.

References

Calvo, G.A. and C.M. Reinhart. "Fear of Floating". *Quarterly Journal of Economics* 107, no. 2 (2002): 379–408.

ECLAC. *Economic Survey of Latin America and the Caribbean: Policies for Creating Quality Jobs*. Santiago de Chile: ECLAC, 2009a.

———. *La reacción de los gobiernos de las Américas frente a la crisis internacional: una presentación sintética de las medidas de política anunciadas hasta el 31 de mayo de 2009*. Santiago de Chile: ECLAC, 2009b.

————. *Cumbre de las Américas 1994–2009. Indicadores seleccionados.* Santiago de Chile: ECLAC, 2009c.

Fernández-Arias, E. and P. Montiel. "Crisis Response in Latin America: Is the 'Rainy Day' at Hand?". Working Paper #686, Inter-American Development Bank, June 2009.

Izquierdo A. and E. Talvi. *Policy Trade-offs for Unprecedented Times: Confronting the Global Crisis in Latin America and the Caribbean.* Inter-American Development Bank, 2008.

Index

www.ingramcontent.com/pod-product-compliance
Lightning Source LLC
Chambersburg PA
CBHW020707270326
41928CB00005B/303